MULTIPLICATION FACTS
THAT STICK

MULTIPLICATION FACTS THAT STICK

Help Your Child Master the Multiplication Facts
for Good in Just Ten Weeks

KATE SNOW

WELL-TRAINED MIND PRESS

TABLE OF CONTENTS

WEEK 4: ×10 FACTS   /   61

WEEK 5: ×5 FACTS   /   67

WEEK 6: ×6 FACTS   /   75

WEEK 7: ×9 FACTS   /   83

WEEK 8: ×7 FACTS / 95

WEEK 9: ×8 FACTS / 103

WEEK 10: REVIEW / 111

GAME BOARDS / 117

PRACTICE PAGES / 197

ANSWER KEYS / 299

PREFACE

When my family visited Rocky Mountain National Park last year, we spent an afternoon at the Alluvial Fan, a 42-acre pile of boulders that tumbled down the mountainside over two decades ago. My two children couldn't wait to try to scramble up this huge rock heap, but I was wary that the climb would be too difficult and tiring for six-year-old Elizabeth. She and I took off towards some of the smaller, easier-to-climb rocks. I figured she'd get worn out quickly, and that we'd turn back after a few minutes. Meanwhile, my husband and nine-year-old son eagerly headed straight up the larger rocks with high hopes of making it to the top.

Elizabeth and I started out tentatively on our climb, always looking for the easiest way possible. Instead of trying to climb directly up the intimidating boulder faces, we looked for small rocks that would gradually boost us up. Step by step, we zigzagged between walls of rock, slowly inching our way higher and higher. It began to drizzle, but we were having so much fun climbing that we didn't even care. After 20 minutes of steady progress, we emerged out of a rocky crevice and discovered that we'd made it to the top of the pile.

Elizabeth beamed with pride as we backtracked down through the rocks. As we descended the final steps, we spotted my husband and son back at the parking lot. It turned out that the sheer rock faces had made them so tired and discouraged that they'd given up and turned back in less than five minutes. Trying to conquer the massive rock pile the hard way had kept them from accomplishing their goal.

In my many years as a math teacher, homeschool parent, tutor, and math curriculum writer, I've found that mastering the multiplication facts can feel as daunting as climbing a pile of boulders. With 100 facts to learn, it's no wonder that parents and children feel like they are facing a mountain of multiplication.

But don't fear! With this book, your child will work steadily and confidently toward mastering the multiplication facts, with lots of success along the way. She will learn the multiplication facts in a logical order, so that she can use easier facts as stepping stones to more difficult facts. And, for each set of facts, she'll play fun games that gently build in difficulty, so that mastering the multiplication facts feels as simple as just taking the next step up—not as difficult as trying to climb straight up a sheer rock face. By the end of the book, your child will have mastered all 100 multiplication facts and feel the glow of triumph that comes from conquering a challenge.

Over the years, I've met so many parents who want to help their children master these important math foundations but just aren't sure how to do so effectively. That's why I've written this book. It will guide you step by step as you help your child master the multiplication facts, once and for all, so that the multiplication facts truly stick.

INTRODUCTION

What makes this approach unique?

~~Practice all the multiplication facts at once.~~

Target one small group of multiplication facts at a time.

Instead of overwhelming your child with all 100 multiplication facts from 1 × 1 up to 10 × 10, this program teaches children just one times table at a time. (A times table is simply one set of multiplication facts. For example, the ×4 table is 1 × 4, 2 × 4, and so on up to 10 × 4.)

1 × 4 = 4
2 × 4 = 8
3 × 4 = 12
4 × 4 = 16
5 × 4 = 20
6 × 4 = 24
7 × 4 = 28
8 × 4 = 32
9 × 4 = 36
10 × 4 = 40

The ×4 times table. Your child will focus on just one times table per week.

Your child will start with the easiest times tables and work his way up to the most difficult ones. Each time he learns a new table, you'll teach him how to use what he's already learned to help him master the new facts. Simple scripted lesson plans are included for each week to guide you every step of the way.

~~Memorize answers.~~

Understand the meaning of the multiplication facts and use easier facts as "stepping stones" to harder facts.

Memorizing answers by rote is time consuming, tedious, and often frustrating. Fortunately, there's a better way!

For example, take 6 × 8. You could have your child learn it by reciting it over and over, copying it out many times, or making up a cute story to remember it. Maybe 6 "ate" 48?

All of this repetition *might* implant 6 × 8 in your child's memory for good. But once he starts to work on 7 × 7 and 7 × 8, will he still remember 6 × 8? And, even if he does remember 6 × 8 permanently, he'll still have 99 more multiplication facts to memorize.

So, what's a better approach? First, children need to understand concretely what each multiplication problem means so that the numbers aren't just sequences of abstract symbols. In our example, 6 × 8 means "six groups of eight." One easy way to make the idea of "six groups of eight" less abstract is to use a simple grid of circles called a dot array.

×	1	2	3	4	5	6	7	8
1	○	○	○	○	○	○	○	○
2	○	○	○	○	○	○	○	○
3	○	○	○	○	○	○	○	○
4	○	○	○	○	○	○	○	○
5	○	○	○	○	○	○	○	○
6	○	○	○	○	○	○	○	○

6 × 8 modeled on a dot array. Each of the six rows has eight dots, so there are six groups of eight.

Second, once your child understands concretely what each multiplication fact means, the dot array will help him use the facts he's already learned to master the harder facts. With rock climbing, it's a lot easier to climb up small rocks gradually rather than try to scale a sheer rock face. With multiplication facts, it's much easier to use facts you've already learned as stepping stones for mastering the harder facts than it may be to memorize them by rote.

For example, even though 6 × 8 is often one of the toughest facts to memorize, most children find it quite easy when they use 5 × 8 as a stepping stone. (5 × 8 makes a nice stepping stone, since children's familiarity with fives from their early years of arithmetic usually make the ×5 facts easy to learn.)

The dot array will help your child visualize how to use 5 × 8 as a stepping stone to 6 × 8:

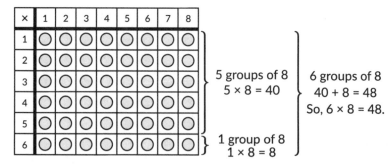

5 × 8 = 40. 6 × 8 is just one more group of eight than 5 × 8. So, you can just add 40 + 8 to find the answer: 6 × 8 = 48.

This combination of the dot array and stepping-stone facts will help your child gradually master all the multiplication facts for good, without having to memorize each fact individually.

~~Drill the multiplication facts over and over.~~

Teach multiplication facts that stick!

Instead of drilling the multiplication facts over and over so that he is exposed to the right answer enough times to memorize it, your child will practice using stepping-stone facts until the answers become automatic. With consistent practice at finding the answers to multiplication problems, your child will get faster and faster—and before long, he will "just know" the answers and have them fully mastered.

HOW TO USE THIS BOOK

Math fact sequence

American math curricula typically teach the math facts as follows:

- Addition facts: 1st grade
- Subtraction facts: 2nd grade
- Multiplication facts: 3rd grade
- Division facts: 4th grade.

No matter what grade your child is in, it's essential that she learn the math facts in this order, because each set of facts builds logically on the previous one. If your child has not yet learned the addition or subtraction facts, have her first work through *Addition Facts That Stick* or *Subtraction Facts That Stick* before you return to this book. Then, once she finishes this book, she'll be ready to move on to *Division Facts That Stick*.

Prerequisite skills

This book is designed for children who have already studied multiplication in a math program, but have not yet memorized the multiplication facts. It is *not* meant to be your child's first exposure to multiplication. Children need a thorough grasp of what multiplication means (for example, that 3 × 8 means "three groups of eight") before they're ready to memorize the facts. You'll review this meaning of multiplication in Week 1, but this brief refresher is not meant to be a substitute for more in-depth study.

While it's fine to use this book to introduce your younger child to the multiplication facts, don't expect thorough mastery of the multiplication facts until your child is *at least* eight years old. Most children's brains aren't developmentally mature enough to memorize all the multiplication facts until this age.

In addition to understanding the meaning of multiplication, your child also needs the following skills to be successful at learning the multiplication facts:

- Understanding the concept of place value. (For example, that five tens and three ones equal 53.)
- Knowing the subtraction facts with a minuend of 10 (10 − 1, 10 − 2, etc. up to 10 − 9).

Weekly overview

You'll teach your child just one times table each week. (The only exception is Week 1, when your child will learn both the ×1 and ×2 tables.) You'll use direct teaching, recitation, games, and written Practice Pages to help your child master the times table each week.

While the goal is for your child to learn one times table per week, please don't feel that you must stick to this exact schedule. All children are unique and learn at their own speed, and you are free to adjust the pacing and activities to best suit your child's needs. (For example, if your child has trouble writing, the Practice Pages can also be done orally—see below.)

Direct teaching

On the first day of each week, you'll teach a short, scripted lesson to introduce the multiplication facts for the week. (During Week 1, you will also review multiplication fundamentals with a quick lesson each day.)

In the lessons, you'll use a ten-by-ten dot array to model multiplication problems, along with an L-shaped paper cover. A dot array is simply a grid of circles that will help your child visualize what the problems mean.

By sliding the L-cover across the dot array, you can model any multiplication problem from 1 × 1 up to 10 × 10. Each lesson will show you how to use the dot array and L-cover to teach your child the multiplication facts for the week. (You can find your own dot array and L-cover on pages 119 and 121. You'll want to pull both pages out of the book for you and your child to use together.)

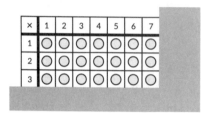

An example of how you'll use the dot array and L-cover to show 3 × 7.

In each lesson, you'll also teach your child how to use the multiplication facts she already knows to help her master new facts.

Recitation

On days 2 through 5, your child will recite the week's times table as a warm-up exercise. Reciting the times tables may seem old-fashioned, but it has several time-tested benefits. First, saying information aloud helps to cement it in your child's memory. Second, reciting each table in order helps your child understand how the facts in the table are related. For example, reciting "1 × 7 is 7. 2 × 7 is 14. 3 × 7 is 21 . . ." reminds your child that each new fact in the ×7 table is seven more than the previous fact. So, she can add seven to each previous fact to help her remember the next one, because the facts in the table add a new group of seven each time.

At the beginning of the week, your child will recite while sliding the L-cover over the dot array. Looking at a visual model of each fact as she recites will give her a visual reminder of how each fact in the table is related to the previous one. It will also help her keep track of where she is in the table. As she becomes more proficient, you'll encourage her to recite the week's times table from memory.

Games

Each day, you and your child will play a game that practices the new facts. These fun games provide a lot of practice in a short amount of time. They also allow you to monitor your child's progress and correct any mistakes right away.

You and your child will play the same five games each week. The games build in difficulty over the course of the week, so that your child steadily becomes more proficient with each new set of multiplication facts. You'll find full directions for each game in the weekly plans, but here's a quick overview of how the games' challenge levels progressively increase.

- Day 1: *Multiplication Race*. In this game, all the answers are visible and arranged in order so that your child can easily pick out the correct answer to each multiplication problem.
- Day 2: *Multiplication Bump*. This game uses the same game board as Day 1's Multiplication Race. However, the spaces on the board are gradually covered so that your child begins to recall the answers from memory.
- Day 3: *Four in a Row*. This tic-tac-toe-like game has all of the answers visible, but they are not arranged in order.
- Day 4: *Roll and Cover*. This game focuses on facts with larger numbers to give these difficult facts some extra practice.
- Day 5: *Over Under*. This game has no printed answers so that your child has to recall all of the answers from memory.

Practice Pages

Your child will also complete a two-sided Practice Page each day. These pages include focused practice of the week's new multiplication facts, along with cumulative review of previous weeks' work.

Many children have difficulties with writing, but there's no reason why writing challenges should hold a child back from mastering the multiplication facts. If your child has dysgraphia or finds writing challenging, have her answer the Practice Page problems orally rather than writing them—simply point to each problem in order and have your child tell you the answer out loud. Younger children may also tire quickly when writing out answers, so feel free to have them solve the problems orally as well.

Teaching tips

- Schedule a consistent time each day for multiplication fact practice. You'll be less likely to forget, and your child will be less likely to argue. Try to choose a time when your child is alert and easily able to concentrate.
- Plan to work on the activities in this book for about 20 minutes each session, with five sessions per week. However, different children need different amounts

of time to master each group of facts. Feel free to take as long as your child needs to master each new set of facts, and don't move on to the new week until your child has the current week's multiplication facts learned.

- The dot array used in the lessons is key to helping children understand the strategies for finding answers. Allow your child to use the dot array whenever she needs it while playing the games and completing the Practice Pages. Then, as she becomes more comfortable with each set of multiplication facts, encourage her to transition to finding the answers mentally, without looking at the array.

- Some math programs teach children to skip-count in order to help them find answers to multiplication problems. (For example, a child might skip-count by 6 seven times to find 7×6: "6, 12, 18, 24, 30, 36, 42.") Rather than skip-counting, encourage your child to use the closest related fact possible to find the answer. (For example, to find 7×6, she might first recall 5×6 and then add two more groups of six.) Using stepping-stone facts is much faster, and it's also less error-prone than skip-counting.

- Keep the practice sessions positive, upbeat, and fast-paced. Have fun playing the games with your child, and enjoy the one-on-one time together.

- Many children freeze when they feel time pressure. Encourage your child to work as efficiently as possible, but don't time her as she does the Practice Pages unless she is aged ten years or older. For an older child, aim for her to know each multiplication fact in three seconds or less.

What you'll need

All of the game boards and Practice Pages you'll need for this program are included in the back of the book. You may want to keep a folder for storing the game boards, in case you want to use them again for review.

Before beginning Week 1, cut out the dot array and L-cover from pages 119 and 121. Prepare the L-cover by cutting along the dotted line and discarding the white rectangle as indicated.

You'll also need a few everyday items to complete the activities and play the games:

- 20 small counters of two different colors (plastic tiles, small blocks, dry beans, coins, etc.)
- Deck of regular playing cards with face cards removed
- Two regular, six-sided dice
- Paper and pencil

WEEK 1

×1 AND ×2
FACTS

WEEK 1 AT A GLANCE

Your child will memorize the ×1 and ×2 facts this week. Even if your child already knows the ×1 and ×2 facts, don't skip this week. In these lessons, you'll review multiplication basics, introduce an important visual model for learning the multiplication facts, and teach your child the rules for the fun games that you both will play throughout the book.

Although it may seem counterintuitive, you'll begin with the ×2 facts before teaching the ×1 facts. That's because the ×2 facts require children to think more deeply about what multiplication means—for example, that 5 × 2 means "five groups of two." With the ×1 facts, it's too easy for children to unthinkingly memorize the answers. To prevent this, you'll start with the ×2 facts so that your child gets into the habit of thinking about the meaning of multiplication right from the outset.

Most weeks, you'll do direct teaching only on Day 1. But with so much material to review this week, you'll teach a short lesson each day so that your child will be well-prepared to tackle the rest of the multiplication facts.

This week, your child will learn these facts:

1 × 1 = 1	1 × 2 = 2
2 × 1 = 2	2 × 2 = 4
3 × 1 = 3	3 × 2 = 6
4 × 1 = 4	4 × 2 = 8
5 × 1 = 5	5 × 2 = 10
6 × 1 = 6	6 × 2 = 12
7 × 1 = 7	7 × 2 = 14
8 × 1 = 8	8 × 2 = 16
9 × 1 = 9	9 × 2 = 18
10 × 1 = 10	10 × 2 = 20

Day 1

Review the Concept of Multiplication

Write **4 × 2 =** on a piece of paper and lay four groups of two counters on the table.

"4 × 2 means four groups of two."

"How many total counters are there in four groups of two?" *Eight.*

"So, since four groups of two is eight, 4 × 2 equals 8." Complete the written multiplication problem: **4 × 2 = 8.**

Write **6 × 2 =** on a piece of paper. "Can you show me this problem with counters?" Your child should lay six groups of two counters on the table. (If he's not sure what to do, prompt him by asking, "How many groups with two counters each would you lay out on the table?" *Six.*)

"How many total counters are there in six groups of two?" *12.* Complete the written multiplication problem: **6 × 2 = 12.**

If your child can easily model the multiplication problem with counters, go on to the next section. If he has trouble, direct him to use the counters to practice modeling each of the following multiplication problems.

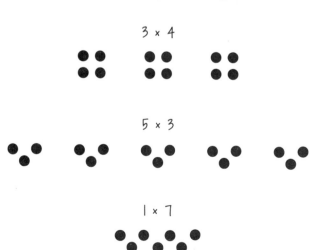

Introduce ×2 facts

Show your child the dot array.

Write **5 × 2 =** on a piece of paper. Slide the L-cover to show five rows of two dots on the array.

"How many rows are showing?" *Five.*

"How many dots are showing in each row?" *Two.*

"How many total dots are showing?" *Ten.*

"We can think of each row as a group. Five rows of two dots is just like five groups of two. So, since ten dots are showing, $5 \times 2 = 10$."

Write **8 × 2 =** on a piece of paper. Have your child slide the L-cover down to match the equation.

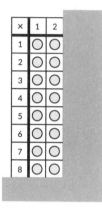

"How many total dots are showing?" *16.*

"So, what does 8 × 2 equal?" *16.*

Have your child complete the written multiplication problem: **8 × 2 = 16.**

Repeat this process with the rest of the ×2 multiplication facts, shown below. Each time, write out the problem. Then, have your child move the L-cover to match the problem and find the answer.

1 × 2 = 2
9 × 2 = 18
3 × 2 = 6
6 × 2 = 12
7 × 2 = 14
10 × 2 = 20
2 × 2 = 4
4 × 2 = 8

Play *Multiplication Race (×2)*

Teach your child how to play *Multiplication Race (×2)* and play.

MATERIALS

- *Multiplication Race/Bump (×2)* game board

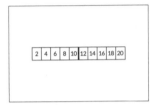

- Deck of cards, with face cards removed (40 cards total)
- Ten small counters per player

OBJECT OF THE GAME

Be the first player to place a counter above or below every number on the game board.

HOW TO PLAY

Shuffle the cards and place them face down in a pile.

To play, you turn over the top card in the deck. Multiply the card's number by two and place one of your counters below the matching number on the game board. For example, if the card is a **6**, place a counter below the **12** on the game board, since 6 × 2 = 12. If the card is an ace, treat it as a 1.

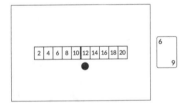

Then ask your child to do the same. When your child plays, have him place his counters *above* the matching number on the game board.

Play until one of you fills all ten spots (either above or below the game board). If you turn over a card and have already placed the matching counter, skip your turn.

Encourage your child to say each multiplication fact out loud as he plays: "7 × 2 is 14." Allow him to use the array and L-cover as needed to find the answers.

Note: Save this game board for tomorrow's game as well.

Independent practice

Have your child complete Practice Pages 1A and 1B in the Week 1 Section. If he has trouble with any of the problems on Practice Page 1B, encourage him to use the dot array and L-cover to help find the answers. Answers are on page 300.

Day 2

Review the commutative property

Write **7 × 2 =** on a piece of paper and slide the L-cover to show seven rows of two.

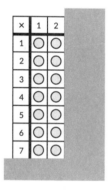

"7 × 2 means seven groups of two. So, what does 7 × 2 equal?" *14.*

Have your child complete the written multiplication problem: **7 × 2 = 14.**

Write **2 × 7 =** just below the previous problem. "If 7 × 2 means seven groups of two, what does 2 × 7 mean?" *Two groups of seven.*

Have your child slide the L-cover to show two rows of seven.

"Now we have two rows of seven instead of seven rows of two. How many dots are showing now?" *14.*

Have your child complete the written multiplication problem: **2 × 7 = 14.**

"Did the total number of dots change when we switched the order of the numbers?" *No.*

"2 × 7 and 7 × 2 have the same *total* number of dots. They just describe the *arrangement* of the dots in two different ways." Rotate the paper a quarter turn to the left to show that the two arrangements are identical.

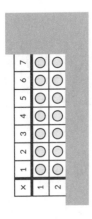

"We can multiply numbers in any order without changing the result. This can make it easier to solve multiplication problems and memorize the multiplication facts."

Write **9 × 2 =** on a piece of paper and slide the L-cover to match.

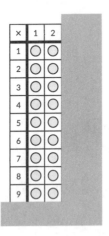

"Adding up nine groups of two can take a while. But since we can multiply numbers in any order, we can change the order of the numbers in the problem and still get the same answer."

Write **2 × 9 =** on a piece of paper and slide the L-cover to match.

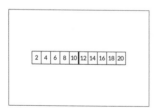

"It's a lot simpler to just add two groups of nine together to find the answer. What's 9 + 9?" *18.*

"So, 2 × 9 and 9 × 2 both equal 18." Have your child complete both of the written multiplication problems: **9 × 2 = 18** and **2 × 9 = 18**.

Repeat this activity with the following pairs of problems to make sure your child understands this important property of multiplication.

$$6 \times 2 = 12 \qquad 8 \times 2 = 16$$
$$2 \times 6 = 12 \qquad 2 \times 8 = 16$$

Play *Multiplication Bump (×2)*

Teach your child how to play *Multiplication Bump (×2)* and play.

MATERIALS

- *Multiplication Race/Bump (×2)* game board

2	4	6	8	10	12	14	16	18	20

- Deck of cards, with face cards removed (40 cards total)
- Ten small counters per player, with a different color for each player

OBJECT OF THE GAME

Cover more spaces on the board than the other player.

HOW TO PLAY

Shuffle the cards and place them face down in a pile.

To play, you begin by turning over the top card in the deck. Multiply the card's number by two and place one of your counters on the matching number on the game board. For example, if the card is a *4*, place a counter on the *8* on the game board, since 4 × 2 = 8.

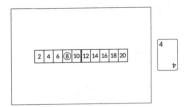

Now ask your child to take a turn.

As the game progresses, if the space containing your answer is already occupied by the other player, "bump" the other player's counter off the space and replace it with your own.

As you play, remind your child to use the commutative property to make it easier to find the answers. For example, to find 7 × 2, he can think of two groups of seven rather than seven groups of two. Also encourage your child to say each multiplication fact out loud as he plays: "8 × 2 is 16."

Play until all ten spots on the game board have been filled. Whoever has more counters on the board at the end wins the game.

Independent practice

Have your child complete Practice Pages 2A and 2B in the Week 1 section. Remind him to complete the times table on Practice Page 2A in order from top to bottom, without skipping around. Also continue to encourage him to use the dot array and L-cover to help him find the answers, if needed. Answers are on page 300.

Day 3

Practice ×2 facts

Use the L-cover to show just one row of two dots on the array.

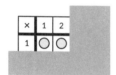

Begin a list of the ×2 facts by writing **1 × 2 =** on a piece of paper. "1 × 2 means one group of two. How many total dots are there?" *Two.*

Have your child complete the written multiplication problem: **1 × 2 = 2.**

Write **2 × 2 =** to continue the list of ×2 facts. Have your child slide the L-cover down to match the equation.

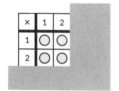

$1 \times 2 = 2$
$2 \times 2 =$

"So, what is 2 × 2?" *Four.*

Have your child complete the written multiplication problem: **2 × 2 = 4.**

Repeat this process with the ×2 multiplication facts in order up to 10 × 2. (They are listed on page 22). Have your child move the L-cover down a row for each new fact so that he connects the visual representation with the spoken and written equations.

Recite ×2 table

"This list we just made is called the 'times two' table. Learning to say the ×2 table will help you memorize these multiplication facts."

Demonstrate how to recite the table. Show one row of two dots on the array and say "1 × 2 is 2." Then, slide the L-cover down and say, "2 × 2 is 4." Continue in this way through 10 × 2.

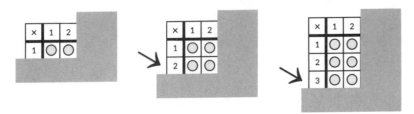

"1 × 2 is 2. 2 × 2 is 4. 3 × 2 is 6 . . ."

Then, ask your child to recite the ×2 table in the same way, sliding the L-cover as he recites so that the dots match each spoken multiplication fact. If your child has trouble keeping track of where he is in the table, prompt him with the next fact: "6 × 2 is?"

Play *Four in a Row (×2)*

Teach your child how to play *Four in a Row (×2)* and play.

MATERIALS

- *Four in a Row (×2)* game board

- Deck of cards, with face cards removed (40 cards total)
- 20 small counters per player, with a different color for each player

OBJECT OF THE GAME

Cover four spaces in a row, either horizontally, vertically, or diagonally.

HOW TO PLAY

Shuffle the cards and place them face down in a pile.

To play, you turn over the top card in the deck. Multiply the card's number by two and place one of your counters on the matching number on the game board. For example, if the card is a *3*, place a counter on the *6* on the game board, since 3 × 2 = 6.

Now ask your child to take a turn.

Encourage your child to say each multiplication fact out loud as he plays: "1 × 2 is 2."

Play until one player covers four spaces in a row on the game board. (The four spaces may be in a row horizontally, vertically, or diagonally.)

Independent practice

Have your child complete Practice Pages 3A and 3B in the Week 1 section. Remind him to complete the times table on Practice Page 3A in order from top to bottom, without skipping around. Answers are on page 301.

Day 4

Warm-up: Recite ×2 table

Have your child recite the ×2 table while sliding the L-cover to match each fact: *1 × 2 is 2. 2 × 2 is 4 . . .*

Practice ×1 facts

"Today we're going to work on the easiest group of multiplication facts: the ×1 facts."

Use the L-cover to show just one dot on the array.

Begin a list of the ×1 facts by writing **1 × 1 =** on a piece of paper. "1 × 1 means one group of one. What does 1 × 1 equal?" *One.*

Have your child complete the written multiplication problem: **1 × 1 = 1.**

Write **2 × 1 =** to continue the list of ×1 facts. Have your child slide the L-cover down to match the equation.

"So, what is 2 × 1?" *Two.*

Have your child complete the written multiplication problem: **2 × 1 = 2.**

Repeat this process with the ×1 multiplication facts in order up to 10 × 1. (They are listed on page 22).

Apply the commutative property to ×1 facts

Write **7 × 1 =** on a piece of paper and slide the L-cover to show seven rows of one.

"What's 7 × 1?" *Seven.*

Have your child complete the written multiplication problem: **7 × 1 = 7.**

Write **1 × 7 =** just below the previous problem. "If 7 × 1 means seven groups of one, what does 1 × 7 mean?" *One group of seven.*

Have your child slide the L-cover to show one row of seven.

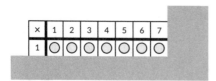

"Now we have one row of seven instead of seven rows of one. How many dots are showing now?" *Seven.*

Have your child complete the written multiplication problem: **1 × 7 = 7.**

"Just like before, the total number of dots stays the same no matter what order we multiply the numbers."

Play *Roll and Cover (×2)*

Teach your child how to play *Roll and Cover (×2)* and play.

MATERIALS

- *Roll and Cover (×2)* game board

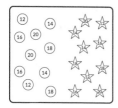

- Two dice
- Ten small counters per player, with a different color for each player

OBJECT OF THE GAME

Cover all the numbers on your side of the game board.

HOW TO PLAY

Have each player choose one side of the game board to cover (either the circles or the stars). Place one die so that five dots are showing. You will not roll this die.

To play, roll the other die. Find the total of both dice. Multiply that total by two and cover the matching number on your side of the game board. For example, if you roll a **3**, cover a **16** on the game board, since 3 + 5 = 8, and 8 × 2 = 16.

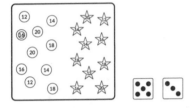

If you roll a **6**, you may cover any space on your side of the game board. If you roll a number that you have already covered, play passes to the other player.

As you play, remind your child that he can use the commutative property of multiplication to make it easier to figure out the problems. For example, to find 7 × 2, he can add together two groups of seven instead of adding up seven groups of two.

Play until one person has covered every number on his side of the game board.

Independent practice

Have your child complete Practice Pages 4A and 4B in the Week 1 section. Remind him to complete the ×1 and ×2 tables on Practice Page 4A in order from top to bottom. Answers are on page 301.

Day 5

Warm-up: Recite ×1 and ×2 tables

Have your child recite the ×1 and ×2 tables. Encourage him to do so from memory, without using the dot array. However, if he has trouble, allow him to use the dot array and L-cover while reciting.

Practice multiplication facts written vertically

Write **6 + 5 = 11** on a piece of paper both horizontally and vertically.

$$6 + 5 = 11 \qquad \begin{array}{r} 6 \\ + 5 \\ \hline 11 \end{array}$$

"When you learned to add, you learned that we can write addition and subtraction problems across the paper horizontally or down the paper vertically. We can write multiplication problems both horizontally and vertically, too."

Write **2 × 5 = 10** on a piece of paper both horizontally and vertically.

$$2 \times 5 = 10 \qquad \begin{array}{r} 2 \\ \times 5 \\ \hline 10 \end{array}$$

"Both of these problems mean the same thing. They're just written two different ways. You'll be solving problems written vertically on your Practice Page today."

Introduce the written multiplication chart

Show your child Practice Page 5A in the Week 1 section.

"This chart organizes all of the multiplication facts from 1 × 1 up to 10 × 10. Each week, you'll complete the parts of the chart that you've learned so far. By the end of the book, you'll know every multiplication fact in the chart!"

"To complete a box, you multiply the number at the beginning of the row by the number at the top of the column." Point to the box shown below.

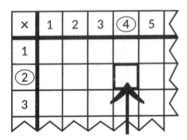

"So, to find the answer that goes in this box, multiply 2 × 4, because *2* is the number for the row and *4* is the number for the column. What's 2 × 4?" *Eight*.

"So, *8* is the answer that goes in this box."

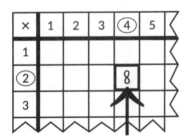

"You'll fill in all the white squares in the chart when you do today's Practice Pages."

Play *Over Under (×2)*

Teach your child how to play *Over Under (×2)* and play.

MATERIALS

- Deck of cards, with face cards removed (40 cards total)
- *Over Under (×2)* game board

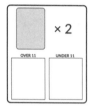

OBJECT OF THE GAME

Win the most cards.

HOW TO PLAY

Place the *Over Under (×2)* game board on the table between the two players. Remove one card from the deck without looking and place it aside. You will not use this card. Shuffle the remaining cards and place them face-down next to the game board. Decide which player is "Over" and which player is "Under."

To play, have your child turn over a card from the pile and place the card face-up in the gray box. Have your child multiply the number on the card by two.

If the answer is less than 11, the player who is "Under" wins the card and places it in the "Under" box. If the answer is greater than 11, the player who is "Over" wins the card and places it in the "Over" box. For example, if your child turns over an *8*, he says, "8 × 2 equals 16," and the player who is "Over" wins the card.

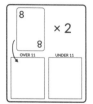

Now, you take a turn, following the same procedure.

Play until you have used all the cards. Whoever wins more cards wins the game.

Independent practice

Have your child complete Practice Pages 5A and 5B in the Week 1 section. (On Practice Page 5A, your child should only fill in the empty white boxes, and not the gray boxes.) Answers are on page 302.

Once your child finishes the Practice Pages, point out that he filled in 36 of the 100 facts in the multiplication chart on Practice Page 5A. After just one week, he already knows over one-third of the facts!

WEEK 2

x3 FACTS

WEEK 2 AT A GLANCE

Your child will use the ×2 facts as stepping stones to mastering the ×3 facts this week. For example, she'll learn to use 2 × 7 to help memorize 3 × 7: since 2 × 7 is two groups of seven, she can add one more group of seven to find that 3 × 7 is 21.

×	1	2	3	4	5	6	7
1	○	○	○	○	○	○	○
2	○	○	○	○	○	○	○
3	○	○	○	○	○	○	○

} 2 groups of 7
2 × 7 = 14

} 1 group of 7
1 × 7 = 7

} 3 groups of 7
14 + 7 = 21
So, 3 × 7 = 21.

To make full use of stepping-stone facts, your child needs to be able to add single-digit numbers to two-digit numbers mentally.

To determine whether or not your child needs more practice with this skill, ask your child to solve the following addition problems mentally:

- 39 + 4? *43.*
- 48 + 6? *54.*
- 63 + 9? *72.*

If your child can solve each problem accurately and within a few seconds, skip the mental addition section in this lesson and move directly to introducing the ×3 facts. You can also skip the mental addition practice exercises that begin each Week 2 lesson.

If your child has trouble with these problems or takes more than a few seconds to solve them, make sure to teach the mental addition section in this lesson and do the practice exercises that are included in the lessons for the rest of the week. Note that you will need two different colors of counters and the ten-frames on page 123 (cut apart on the dotted lines).

This week, your child will learn these facts:

1 × 3 = 3	6 × 3 = 18
2 × 3 = 6	7 × 3 = 21
3 × 3 = 9	8 × 3 = 24
4 × 3 = 12	9 × 3 = 27
5 × 3 = 15	10 × 3 = 30

Day 1

Practice mental addition (if needed—see page 42)

"This week, you're going to learn the ×3 multiplication facts. You'll need to use addition as you figure out these facts, so we're going to practice some addition first."

Write **29 + 3 =** on a piece of paper. "We'll use ten-frames and counters to show this problem. A ten-frame is just a grid with ten dots in it, like the rows in the dot array."

"Instead of using 29 counters to show the problem, we're going to save time and use two ten-frames that are already filled in. Each dot in a ten-frame stands for a counter." Place two full ten-frames and one empty ten-frame on the table. Fill the empty ten-frame with nine counters from left to right.

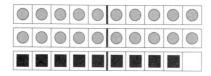

"There are two tens, plus nine more counters, for a total of 29. Now, we need to add three." Place three counters of another color next to the ten-frames.

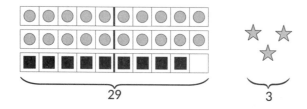

"Let's fill in the empty spot in the ten-frame to make it easier to see the answer to the problem." Move one loose counter to the empty spot in the ten-frame.

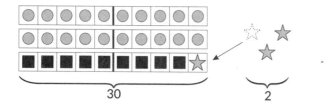

"How many tens are filled in now?" *Three.*

"How many loose counters are there?" *Two.*

"So, what's 29 + 3?" *32.* (If your child's not sure, ask, "What do the three tens equal?" *30.* "So, what's 30 + 2?" *32.)*

Repeat this process with the following problems. Each time, have her complete the empty boxes in the partially-full ten-frame to make it easier to find the answer.

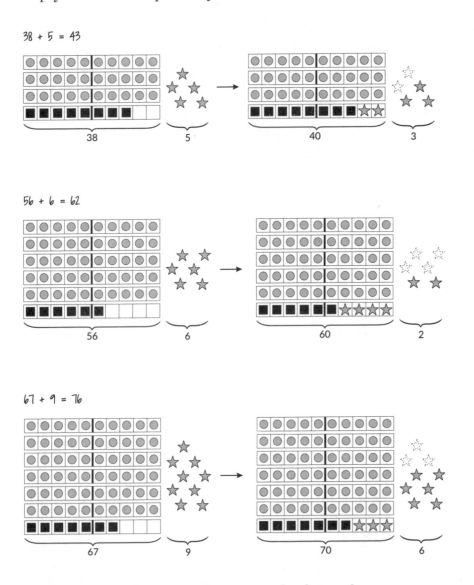

Save the ten-frames and counters for future lessons.

Note: This lesson is meant to be an introduction to mental addition, and it's not expected that your child will master it after just one practice session. She will become more skillful as she practices mental addition at the beginning of each lesson this week. Also, it's fine if your child is able to solve the problems without the ten-frames, or if she uses a different approach to find the answers. What matters most is that she learns to quickly and confidently add a two-digit number to a one-digit number so that she's able to use addition to master the multiplication facts.

Introduce ×3 facts

"Now, we'll start on the ×3 multiplication facts."

Use the L-cover to show one row of three dots on the dot array.

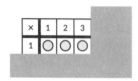

Begin a list of the ×3 facts by writing **1 × 3 =** on a piece of paper. "1 × 3 means one group of three. How many total dots are there?" *Three.*

Have your child complete the written multiplication problem: **1 × 3 = 3.**

Write **2 × 3 =** to continue the list of ×3 facts. Have your child slide the L-cover down to match the equation.

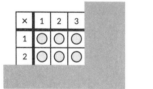

"So, what is 2 × 3?" *Six.*

Have your child complete the written multiplication problem: **2 × 3 = 6.**

Repeat this process with the ×3 multiplication facts in order up to 10 × 3. (They are listed on page 42). Have your child slide the L-cover down a row for each new fact so that she connects the visual representation with the spoken and written equations.

Use the ×2 facts to learn the ×3 facts

Write **6 × 3 =** and **3 × 6 =** on a piece of paper.

"Since we can multiply in any order without changing the result, we can solve either problem to find the answer to both."

"It's often faster to add up three groups of six rather than six groups of three. That's because you can use a multiplication fact you've already learned to help you find the answer quickly."

Write **2 × 6 =** on a piece of paper and slide the L-cover to match.

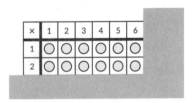

"2 × 6 is two groups of six. What's 2 × 6?" *12.*

"3 × 6 is just one more group of six. So, you can add six more to 12 to find the answer to 3 × 6." Slide the L-cover down a row so that three rows of six show.

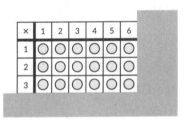

"What's 6 + 12?" *18.*

So, what's the answer to 3 × 6?" *18.*

Have your child complete the written multiplication problem: **3 × 6 = 18.**

Repeat this activity with the following problems.

2 × 7 = 14   2 × 9 = 18
3 × 7 = 21   3 × 9 = 27

2 × 10 = 20   2 × 8 = 16
3 × 10 = 30   3 × 8 = 24

Play *Multiplication Race (×3)*

Play *Multiplication Race (×3).* Use the same directions as in Week 1, but use the *Multiplication Race/Bump (×3)* game board (page 133) and multiply each card by three, rather than by two. For example, if you turn over a **6**, place a counter below the **18** on the game board, since 6 × 3 = 18.

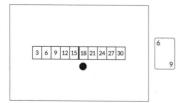

Note: Save this game board for tomorrow's game as well.

Independent practice

Have your child complete Practice Pages 1A and 1B in the Week 2 section. On Practice Page 1A, remind your child to complete the times tables in order from top to bottom. (She should always do this when completing times tables throughout the rest of the book, although the direction will not be repeated.) Also, on Practice Page 1B, encourage her to use each ×2 fact as a stepping stone to finding the answer to the ×3 fact below it. Answers are on page 302.

Day 2

Mental addition practice (if needed—see page 42)

Have your child use the ten-frames and counters to solve the following problems. Use the same process as in Day 1, and remind your child to fill in the empty boxes in the ten-frame to help find each answer.

79 + 6 = 85

45 + 7 = 52

58 + 4 = 62

Warm-up: Recite ×3 table

Demonstrate how to recite the ×3 table. First, show one row of three dots on the dot array and say "1 × 3 is 3." Then, slide the L-cover down one row and say, "2 × 3 is 6." Continue in this way through 10 × 3.

Then, ask your child to recite the ×3 table in the same way. Have her slide the L-cover so that the dots match each spoken multiplication fact. If your child has trouble keeping track of where she is in the table, prompt her with the next fact, such as: "5 × 3 is . . .?"

Play *Multiplication Bump (×3)*

Play *Multiplication Bump (×3)*. Use the same directions as in Week 1, but use the *Multiplication Race/Bump (×3)* game board (page 133) and multiply each card by three, rather than by two. For example, if the card is a **4**, place a counter on the **12** on the game board, since 4 × 3 = 12.

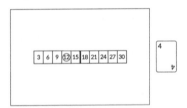

As you play, remind your child to use ×2 facts as stepping stones to finding the answers to ×3 facts.

Independent practice

Have your child complete Practice Pages 2A and 2B in the Week 2 section. Answers are on page 303.

Day 3

Mental addition practice (if needed—see page 42)

Have your child use the ten-frames and counters to solve the following problems. Use the same process as in Day 1, and remind your child to fill in the empty boxes in the ten-frame to help find each answer.

$$68 + 4 = 72$$
$$57 + 6 = 63$$
$$26 + 9 = 35$$

Warm-up: Recite ×3 table

Have your child recite the ×3 table while sliding the L-cover to match each fact: *1 × 3 is 3. 2 × 3 is 6 . . .*

Play *Four in a Row (×3)*

Play *Four in a Row (×3)*. Use the same directions as in Week 1, but use the *Four in a Row (×3)* game board (page 135) and multiply each card by three, rather than by two. For example, if the card is a *3*, place a counter on the *9* on the game board, since 3 × 3 = 9.

Independent practice

Have your child complete Practice Pages 3A and 3B in the Week 2 section. Answers are on page 303.

Day 4

Mental addition practice (if needed—see page 46)

Have your child use the ten-frames and counters to solve the following problems. Use the same process as in Day 1, and remind your child to fill in the empty boxes in the ten-frame to help find each answer.

$19 + 5 = 24$

$46 + 6 = 52$

$35 + 8 = 43$

Warm-up: Recite ×3 table

Have your child recite the ×3 table. Encourage her to do so from memory, without using the dot array. However, if she has trouble, allow her to use the dot array and L-cover while reciting.

Play *Roll and Cover (×3)*

Play *Roll and Cover (×3)*. Use the same directions as in Week 1, but use the *Roll and Cover (×3)* game board (page 137) and multiply the total of the dice by three, rather than by two. For example, if you roll a *4*, cover the *27* on the game board, since $5 + 4 = 9$, and $9 \times 3 = 27$.

Independent practice

Have your child complete Practice Pages 4A and 4B in the Week 2 section. Answers are on page 304.

Day 5

Mental addition practice (if needed—see page 42)

Have your child use the ten-frames and counters to solve the following problems. Use the same process as in Day 1, and remind your child to fill in the empty boxes in the ten-frame to help find each answer.

$$36 + 4 = 40$$
$$49 + 9 = 58$$
$$65 + 7 = 72$$

Warm-up: Recite ×3 table

Have your child recite the ×3 table. If she has trouble recalling the facts from memory, allow her to use the L-cover and dot array while reciting.

Play *Over Under (×3)*

Play *Over Under (×3)*. Use the same directions as in Week 1, but use the *Over Under (×3)* game board (page 139) and multiply the number on the card by three, rather than by two.

If the answer is less than 16, the player who is "Under" wins the card and places it in the "Under" box. If the answer is greater than 16, the player who is "Over" wins the card and places it in the "Over" box. For example, if your child turns over a **7**, she says, "7 × 3 equals 21," and the player who is "Over" wins the card.

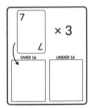

Independent practice

Have your child complete Practice Pages 5A and 5B in the Week 2 section. (On Practice Page 5A, your child should only fill in the empty white boxes, and not the gray boxes.) Answers are on page 304.

Once your child finishes the Practice Pages, point out that she has filled in 51 of the 100 facts in the multiplication chart on Practice Page 5A. She's already learned over half the facts!

WEEK 3

×4 FACTS

WEEK 3 AT A GLANCE

As he did last week, your child will use the ×2 facts as a stepping stone. This week, he'll find the answers to the ×4 facts by doubling the related ×2 facts. For example, he'll learn to use 2×6 to find 4×6: since 2×6 is two groups of six, he can double 12 to find that 4×6 equals 24.

×	1	2	3	4	5	6

2 groups of 6
$2 \times 6 = 12$

2 groups of 6
$2 \times 6 = 12$

4 groups of 6
$12 + 12 = 24$
So, $4 \times 6 = 24$.

This week, your child will learn these facts:

$1 \times 4 = 4$

$2 \times 4 = 8$

$3 \times 4 = 12$

$4 \times 4 = 16$

$5 \times 4 = 20$

$6 \times 4 = 24$

$7 \times 4 = 28$

$8 \times 4 = 32$

$9 \times 4 = 36$

$10 \times 4 = 40$

Day 1

Introduce ×4 facts

"This week, you're going to learn the ×4 multiplication facts."

Use the L-cover to show just one row of four dots on the dot array.

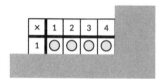

Begin a list of the ×4 facts by writing **1 × 4 =** on a piece of paper. "1 × 4 means one group of four. How many total dots are there?" *Four.*

Have your child complete the written multiplication problem: **1 × 4 = 4.**

Write **2 × 4 =** to continue the list of ×4 facts. Have your child slide the L-cover down to match the equation.

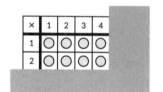

$1 \times 4 = 4$
$2 \times 4 =$

"So, what is 2 × 4?" *Eight.* Remind your child that he can add 4 + 4 to find the answer if he's not sure.

Have your child complete the written multiplication problem: **2 × 4 = 8.**

Repeat this process with the ×4 multiplication facts in order up to 10 × 4. (They are listed on page 54). Have your child move the L-cover down a row for each new fact so that he connects the visual representation with the spoken and written equations.

Use the ×2 facts to find ×4 facts

Write **7 × 4 =** and **4 × 7 =** on a piece of paper.

"Since we can multiply in any order without changing the result, we can solve either problem to find the answer to both."

"It's usually faster to add up four groups of seven rather than seven groups of four. Just like with the ×3 facts, you can use a multiplication fact you've already learned to help you find the answer quickly."

Write **2 × 7 =** on a piece of paper and slide the L-cover to match.

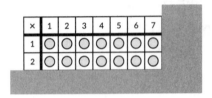

"What's 2 × 7?" *14.*

"4 × 7 is twice as much as 2 × 7." Slide the L-cover down two rows so that four rows of seven show.

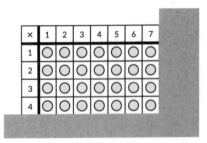

"So, you can just double 14 to find the answer to 4 × 7. What's double 14?" *28.*

"So, what's the answer to 4 × 7?" *28.*

Have your child complete the written multiplication problem: **4 × 7 = 28.**

Repeat this activity with the following pairs of problems.

2 × 5 = 10   2 × 9 = 18
4 × 5 = 20   4 × 9 = 36

2 × 10 = 20   2 × 8 = 16
4 × 10 = 40   4 × 8 = 32

Play *Multiplication Race (×4)*

Play *Multiplication Race (×4)*. Use the same directions as in Week 1, but use the *Multiplication Race/Bump (×4)* game board (page 141) and multiply each card by four, rather than by two. For example, if the card is a *5*, place a counter below the *20* on the game board, since 5 × 4 = 20.

Note: Save this game board for tomorrow's game as well.

Independent practice

Have your child complete Practice Pages 1A and 1B in the Week 3 section. On Practice Page 1B, remind your child to use each ×2 fact as a stepping stone to finding the answer to the ×4 fact below it. Answers are on page 305.

Day 2

Warm-up: Recite ×4 table

Have your child recite the ×4 table while sliding the L-cover to match each fact: *1 × 4 is 4. 2 × 4 is 8 . . .*

Play *Multiplication Bump (×4)*

Play *Multiplication Bump (×4)*. Use the same directions as in Week 1, but use the *Multiplication Race/Bump (×4)* game board (page 141) and multiply each card by four, rather than by two. For example, if the card is a *3*, place a counter on the *12* on the game board, since 3 × 4 = 12.

As you play, remind your child to use ×2 facts as stepping stones to finding the answer to ×4 facts.

Independent practice

Have your child complete Practice Pages 2A and 2B in the Week 3 section. Answers are on page 305.

Day 3

Warm-up: Recite ×4 table

Have your child recite the ×4 table while sliding the L-cover to match each fact: *1 × 4 is 4. 2 × 4 is 8 . . .*

Play *Four in a Row (×4)*

Play *Four in a Row (×4)*. Use the same directions as in Week 1, but use the *Four in a Row (×4)* game board (page 143) and multiply each card by four, rather than by two. For example, if the card is a **10**, place a counter on the **40** on the game board, since 10 × 4 = 10.

Independent practice

Have your child complete Practice Pages 3A and 3B in the Week 3 section. Answers are on page 306.

Day 4

Warm-up: Recite ×4 table

Have your child recite the ×4 table. Encourage him to do so from memory, without using the dot array. However, if he has trouble, allow him to use the dot array and L-cover while reciting.

Play *Roll and Cover (×4)*

Play *Roll and Cover (×4)*. Use the same directions as in Week 1, but use the *Roll and Cover (×4)* game board (page 145) and multiply the total of the dice by four, rather than by two. For example, if you roll a *4*, cover the *36* on the game board, since 4 + 5 = 9, and 9 × 4 = 36.

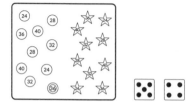

Independent practice

Have your child complete Practice Pages 4A and 4B in the Week 3 section. Answers are on page 306.

Day 5

Warm-up: Recite ×4 table

Have your child recite the ×4 table. If he has trouble recalling the facts from memory, allow him to use the L-cover and dot array while reciting.

Play *Over Under (×4)*

Play *Over Under (×4)*. Use the same directions as in Week 1, but use the *Over Under (×4)* game board (page 147) and multiply the number on the card by four, rather than by two.

If the answer is less than 22, the player who is "Under" wins the card and places it in the "Under" box. If the answer is greater than 22, the player who is "Over" wins the card and places it in the "Over" box. For example, if your child turns over a *2*, he says, "2 × 4 equals 8," and the player who is "Under" wins the card.

Independent practice

Have your child complete Practice Pages 5A and 5B in the Week 3 section. (On Practice Page 5A, your child should only fill in the empty white boxes, and not the gray boxes.) Answers are on page 307.

Once your child finishes the Practice Pages, point out that he filled in 64 of the 100 facts in the multiplication chart on Practice Page 5A. Only 36 left to learn!

WEEK 4

x10 FACTS

WEEK 4 AT A GLANCE

You will skip ahead to the ×10 facts this week. Most children find these facts quite easy to memorize, and learning them now will make it easier for your child to master the ×5 facts next week.

Your child will use her understanding of place value to master the ×10 facts. For example, since 7×10 means seven groups of ten, and since place value tells us that 70 equals seven tens, 7×10 equals 70.

×	1	2	3	4	5	6	7	8	9	10
1	○	○	○	○	○	○	○	○	○	○
2	○	○	○	○	○	○	○	○	○	○
3	○	○	○	○	○	○	○	○	○	○
4	○	○	○	○	○	○	○	○	○	○
5	○	○	○	○	○	○	○	○	○	○
6	○	○	○	○	○	○	○	○	○	○
7	○	○	○	○	○	○	○	○	○	○

7 groups of 10
7 tens is 70.
So, $7 \times 10 = 70$.

This week, your child will learn these facts:

$1 \times 10 = 10$
$2 \times 10 = 20$
$3 \times 10 = 30$
$4 \times 10 = 40$
$5 \times 10 = 50$
$6 \times 10 = 60$
$7 \times 10 = 70$
$8 \times 10 = 80$
$9 \times 10 = 90$
$10 \times 10 = 100$

Day 1

Introduce ×10 facts

"This week, you're going to learn the ×10 multiplication facts."

Have your child help you make a list of the ×10 multiplication facts up to 10 × 10 = 100, just as in previous weeks. For each multiplication fact, write out the multiplication problem, slide the L-cover to match the problem, and then have your child answer the problem.

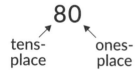

$1 \times 10 = 10$
$2 \times 10 = 20$
$3 \times 10 = 30$
⋮

Use place value to remember ×10 facts

"You can use what you know about place value to help you remember the ×10 facts."

Write **80** on a piece of paper.

"In the number 80, the *8* is in the tens-place and the *0* is in the ones-place. That means that there are eight tens and zero ones in 80."

80

tens-
place

ones-
place

Write **8 × 10 = 80** on a piece of paper.

"8 × 10 means eight groups of ten. Eight tens equals 80, so we know right away that the answer has to be 80."

Have your child use the same reasoning to find the answers to the following problems.

$6 \times 10 = 60$

$9 \times 10 = 90$

$4 \times 10 = 40$

Play *Multiplication Race (×10)*

Play *Multiplication Race (×10)*. Use the same directions as in Week 1, but use the *Multiplication Race/Bump (×10)* game board (page 189) and multiply each card by ten, rather than by two.

Note: Save this game board for tomorrow's game as well.

Independent practice

Have your child complete Practice Pages 1A and 1B in the Week 4 section. Answers are on page 307.

Day 2

Warm-up: Recite ×10 table

Have your child recite the ×10 table while sliding the L-cover to match each fact: *1 × 10 is 10. 2 × 10 is 20 . . .*

Play *Multiplication Bump (×10)*

Play *Multiplication Bump (×10)*. Use the same directions as in Week 1, but use the *Multiplication Race/Bump (×10)* game board (page 189) and multiply each card by ten, rather than by two.

Independent practice

Have your child complete Practice Pages 2A and 2B in the Week 4 section. Answers are on page 308.

Day 3

Warm-up: Recite ×10 table

Have your child recite the ×10 table while sliding the L-cover to match each fact. *1 × 10 is 10. 2 × 10 is 20 . . .*

Play *Four in a Row (×10)*

Play *Four in a Row (×10)*. Use the same directions as in Week 1, but use the *Four in a Row (×10)* game board (page 191) and multiply each card by ten, rather than by two.

Independent practice

Have your child complete Practice 3A and 3B in the Week 4 section. Answers are on page 308.

Day 4

Warm-up: Recite ×10 table

Have your child recite the ×10 table. Encourage her to do so from memory, without using the dot array. However, if she has trouble, allow her to use the dot array and L-cover while reciting.

Play *Roll and Cover (×10)*

Play *Roll and Cover (×10)*. Use the same directions as in Week 1, but use the *Roll and Cover (×10)* game board (page 193) and multiply the total of the dice by ten, rather than by two. For example, if you roll a *1*, cover the *60* on the game board, since 1 + 5 = 6, and 6 × 10 = 60.

Independent practice

Have your child complete Practice Pages 4A and 4B in the Week 4 section. Answers are on page 309.

Day 5

Warm-up: Recite ×10 table

Have your child recite the ×10 table. If she has trouble recalling the facts from memory, allow her to use the L-cover and dot array while reciting.

Play *Over Under (×10)*

Play *Over Under (×10)*. Use the same directions as in Week 1, but use the *Over Under (×10)* game board (page 195) and multiply the number on the card by ten, rather than by two.

If the answer is less than 55, the player who is "Under" wins the card and places it in the "Under" box. If the answer is greater than 55, the player who is "Over" wins the card and places it in the "Over" box.

Independent practice

Have your child complete Practice Pages 5A and 5B in the Week 4 section. Answers are on page 309.

Once your child finishes the Practice Pages, point out that she has learned 75 of the 100 facts in the multiplication chart on Practice Page 5A.

WEEK 5

x5 FACTS

WEEK 5 AT A GLANCE

Now that your child has learned the ×10 facts, he'll build on that knowledge to memorize the ×5 facts this week. He will learn to find the answers by putting together two groups of five to make a ten. For example, to find 6 × 5, he'll think, "Every two groups of five makes ten. Since I have six groups of five, I can make three tens. Three tens is 30, so 6 × 5 is 30."

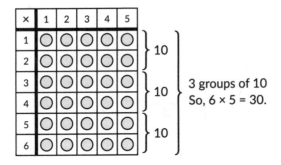

This week, your child will learn these facts:

$1 \times 5 = 5$

$2 \times 5 = 10$

$3 \times 5 = 15$

$4 \times 5 = 20$

$5 \times 5 = 25$

$6 \times 5 = 30$

$7 \times 5 = 35$

$8 \times 5 = 40$

$9 \times 5 = 45$

$10 \times 5 = 50$

Day 1

Introduce ×5 facts

"This week, you're going to learn the ×5 multiplication facts."

Use the L-cover to show just one row of five dots on the dot array.

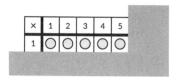

Begin a list of the ×5 facts by writing **1 × 5 =** on a piece of paper. "1 × 5 means one group of five. What's 1 × 5?" *5.*

Have your child complete the written multiplication problem: **1 × 5 = 5.**

Write **2 × 5 =** to continue the list of ×5 facts. Have your child slide the L-cover down to match the equation.

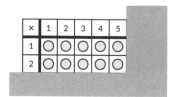

$1 \times 5 = 5$
$2 \times 5 =$

"So, what is 2 × 5?" *Ten.*

Have your child complete the written multiplication problem: **2 × 5 = 10.**

"We can use the fact that two groups of five equal ten to make learning the rest of the ×5 table easier."

Repeat this process with **3 × 5 = 15.**

For **4 × 5 = 20**, ask, "How can you use groups of ten to make it easier to find the answer?" *Sample answer: I can add together the four groups of five to make two groups of ten.*

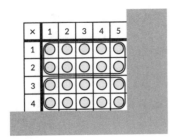

Have your child complete the written multiplication problem: **4 × 5 = 20.**

Repeat this process with the rest of the ×5 multiplication facts in order up to 10 × 5. (They are listed on page 68). As your child figures out the answers, remind him to add together groups of five to make tens whenever possible.

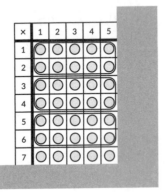

Encourage your child to think of 7 × 5 as three groups of ten, plus one more group of five.

Play *Multiplication Race* (×5)

Play *Multiplication Race (×5)*. Use the same directions as in Week 1, but use the *Multiplication Race/Bump (×5)* game board (page 149) and multiply each card by five, rather than by two. For example, if the card is a **6**, place a counter below the **30** on the game board, since 6 × 5 = 30.

Note: Save this game board for tomorrow's game as well.

Independent practice

Have your child complete Practice Pages 1A and 1B in the Week 5 section. Answers are on page 310.

Day 2

Warm-up: Recite ×5 table

Have your child recite the ×5 table while sliding the L-cover to match each fact: *1 × 5 is 5. 2 × 5 is 10 . . .*

Play *Multiplication Bump (×5)*

Play *Multiplication Bump (×5)*. Use the same directions as in Week 1, but use the *Multiplication Race/Bump (×5)* game board (page 149) and multiply each card by five, rather than by two.

Independent practice

Have your child complete Practice Pages 2A and 2B in the Week 5 section. Answers are on page 310.

Day 3

Warm-up: Recite ×5 table

Have your child recite the ×5 table while sliding the L-cover to match each fact: *1 × 5 is 5. 2 × 5 is 10 . . .*

Play *Four in a Row (×5)*

Play *Four in a Row (×5)*. Use the same directions as in Week 1, but use the *Four in a Row (×5)* game board (page 151) and multiply each card by five, rather than by two.

Independent practice

Have your child complete Practice Pages 3A and 3B in the Week 5 section. Answers are on page 311.

Day 4

Warm-up: Recite ×5 table

Have your child recite the ×5 table. Encourage him to do so from memory, without using the dot array. However, if he has trouble, allow him to use the dot array and L-cover while reciting.

Play *Roll and Cover (×5)*

Play *Roll and Cover (×5)*. Use the same directions as in Week 1, but use the *Roll and Cover (×5)* game board (page 153) and multiply the total of the dice by five, rather than by two. For example, if you roll a *3*, cover the *40* on the game board, since 3 + 5 = 8, and 8 × 5 = 40.

Independent practice

Have your child complete Practice Pages 4A and 4B in the Week 5 section. Answers are on page 311.

Day 5

Warm-up: Recite ×5 table

Have your child recite the ×5 table. If he has trouble recalling the facts from memory, allow him to use the L-cover and dot array while reciting.

Play *Over Under (×5)*

Play *Over Under (×5)*. Use the same directions as in Week 1, but use the *Over Under (×5)* game board (page 155) and multiply the number on the card by five, rather than by two.

If the answer is less than 28, the player who is "Under" wins the card and places it in the "Under" box. If the answer is greater than 28, the player who is "Over" wins the card and places it in the "Over" box.

Independent practice

Have your child complete Practice Pages 5A and 5B in the Week 5 section. (On Practice Page 5A, your child should only fill in the empty white boxes, and not the gray boxes.) Answers are on page 312.

Once your child finishes the Practice Pages, point out that he has learned 84 of the 100 facts in the multiplication chart on Practice Page 5A. Only 16 facts left!

WEEK 6

x6 FACTS

WEEK 6 AT A GLANCE

Your child will use the ×5 facts as a stepping stone to mastering the ×6 facts this week. For example, she'll learn to use 5×7 to help memorize 6×7: since 6×7 is just one more group of seven than 5×7, she can add seven to 35 to find that 6×7 is 42.

5 groups of 7
$5 \times 7 = 35$

1 group of 7
$1 \times 7 = 7$

6 groups of 7
$35 + 7 = 42$
So, $6 \times 7 = 42$.

This week, your child will learn these facts:

$1 \times 6 = 6$
$2 \times 6 = 12$
$3 \times 6 = 18$
$4 \times 6 = 24$
$5 \times 6 = 30$
$6 \times 6 = 36$
$7 \times 6 = 42$
$8 \times 6 = 48$
$9 \times 6 = 54$
$10 \times 6 = 60$

Day 1

Introduce ×6 facts

"This week, you're going to learn the ×6 multiplication facts."

Have your child help you make a list of the ×6 multiplication facts up to $10 \times 6 = 60$, just as in previous weeks. For each multiplication fact, write out the multiplication problem, slide the L-cover to match the problem, and then have your child answer the problem.

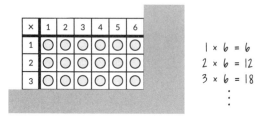

$1 \times 6 = 6$
$2 \times 6 = 12$
$3 \times 6 = 18$
$\vdots$

Use the ×5 facts to find ×6 facts

"You've learned that we can multiply in any order without changing the answer. We can use that fact along with the ×5 facts to make it easier to figure out the ×6 facts."

Write **5 × 7 =** on a piece of paper and slide the L-cover to match.

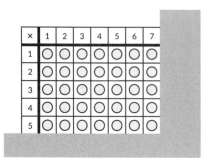

Have your child complete the written multiplication problem: **5 × 7 = 35.**
Write **6 × 7 =** directly below **5 × 7 = 35.**

"6 × 7 is just one more group of seven. So, you can add seven more to 35 to find the answer to 6 × 7." Slide the L-cover down a row to show one more row of seven dots.

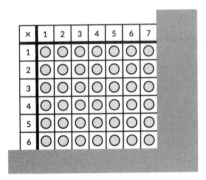

"So, what's 6 × 7?" *42.*

Have your child complete the written multiplication problem: **6 x 7 = 42.**

Repeat this activity with the following pairs of problems. Encourage your child to use each ×5 fact as a stepping stone to the related ×6 fact.

$$5 \times 4 = 20 \qquad 5 \times 9 = 45$$
$$6 \times 4 = 24 \qquad 6 \times 9 = 54$$

$$5 \times 8 = 40 \qquad 5 \times 6 = 30$$
$$6 \times 8 = 48 \qquad 6 \times 6 = 36$$

Play *Multiplication Race (×6)*

Play *Multiplication Race (×6).* Use the same directions as in Week 1, but use the *Multiplication Race/Bump (×6)* game board (page 157) and multiply each card by six rather than by two.

Note: Save this game board for tomorrow's game as well.

Independent practice

Have your child complete Practice Pages 1A and 1B in the Week 6 section. On Practice Page 1B, remind your child to use each ×5 fact as a stepping stone to finding the answer to the ×6 fact below it. Answers are on page 312.

Day 2

Warm-up: Recite ×6 table

Have your child recite the ×6 table while sliding the L-cover to match each fact: *1 × 6 is 6. 2 × 6 is 12 . . .*

Play *Multiplication Bump (×6)*

Play *Multiplication Bump (×6)*. Use the same directions as in Week 1, but use the *Multiplication Race/Bump (×6)* game board (page 157) and multiply each card by six, rather than by two.

As you play, remind your child to use ×5 facts as stepping stones to finding the answer to the ×6 facts.

Independent practice

Have your child complete Practice Pages 2A and 2B in the Week 6 section. Answers are on page 313.

Day 3

Warm-up: Recite ×6 table

Have your child recite the ×6 table while sliding the L-cover to match each fact: *1 × 6 is 6. 2 × 6 is 12 . . .*

Play *Four in a Row (×6)*

Play *Four in a Row (×6)*. Use the same directions as in Week 1, but use the *Four in a Row (×6)* game board (page 159) and multiply each card by six, rather than by two.

Independent practice

Have your child complete Practice Pages 3A and 3B in the Week 6 section. Answers are on page 313.

Day 4

Warm-up: Recite ×6 table

Have your child recite the ×6 table. Encourage her to do so from memory, without using the dot array. However, if she has trouble, allow her to use the dot array and L-cover while reciting.

Play *Roll and Cover (×6)*

Play *Roll and Cover (×6)*. Use the same directions as in Week 1, but use the *Roll and Cover (×6)* game board (page 161) and multiply the total of the dice by six, rather than by two. For example, if you roll a *2*, cover a *42* on the game board, since 2 + 5 = 7, and 7 × 6 = 42.

Independent practice

Have your child complete Practice Pages 4A and 4B in the Week 6 section. Answers are on page 314.

Day 5

Warm-up: Recite ×6 table

Have your child recite the ×6 table. If she has trouble recalling the facts from memory, allow her to use the L-cover and dot array while reciting.

Play *Over Under (×6)*

Play *Over Under (×6)*. Use the same directions as in Week 1, but use the *Over Under (×6)* game board (page 163) and multiply the number on the card by six, rather than by two.

If the answer is less than 32, the player who is "Under" wins the card and places it in the "Under" box. If the answer is greater than 32, the player who is "Over" wins the card and places it in the "Over" box.

Independent practice

Have your child complete Practice Pages 5A and 5B in the Week 6 section. Answers are on page 314.

Once your child finishes the Practice Pages, point out that she has learned 91 of the 100 facts in the multiplication chart on Practice Page 5A. Fewer than ten facts to go!

WEEK 7

x9 FACTS

WEEK 7 AT A GLANCE

Your child will memorize the ×9 facts this week. However, because of the commutative property, he has already learned most of the ×9 facts in the previous weeks. (For example, he learned 3 × 9 along with 9 × 3 during Week 2, and he learned 5 × 9 and 9 × 5 in Week 4.) He will practice the ×9 facts that he's already learned some more this week.

Only three new ×9 facts remain for your child to learn: 7 × 9, 8 × 9, and 9 × 9. For these facts, he'll use the ×10 facts as stepping stones to mastery. For example, he'll learn to use 10 × 8 to find 9 × 8. Since 9 × 8 is just one fewer group of eight than 10 × 8, he can subtract one group of eight from 80 to find that 9 × 8 is 72.

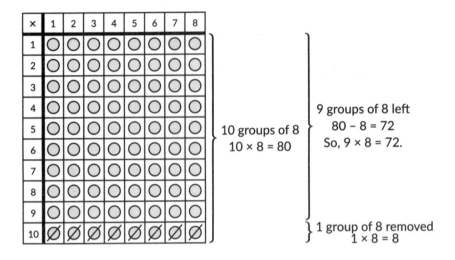

To make full use of this strategy, your child needs to be able to subtract single-digit numbers from multiples of ten (numbers like 50, 70, or 20). To determine whether or not your child needs more practice with this skill, ask him to solve the following subtraction problems mentally:

- 30 – 4? *26.*
- 40 – 3? *37.*
- 70 – 9? *61.*

If your child can solve each problem accurately and within a few seconds, skip the mental subtraction section in this lesson and move directly to introducing the ×9 facts. You can also skip the mental subtraction practice exercises that begin the Week 7 lessons.

If your child has trouble with these problems or takes more than a few seconds to solve them, make sure to teach the mental subtraction section in this lesson and do the practice exercises included in the rest of this week's lessons. Note that you will need the ten-frames from page 123 (cut apart on the dotted lines) and a blank piece of paper for these lessons.

This week, your child will learn these facts:

$1 \times 9 = 9$

$2 \times 9 = 18$

$3 \times 9 = 27$

$4 \times 9 = 36$

$5 \times 9 = 45$

$6 \times 9 = 54$

$7 \times 9 = 63$

$8 \times 9 = 72$

$9 \times 9 = 81$

$10 \times 9 = 90$

Day 1

Practice mental subtraction (if needed—see page 84)

"This week, you're going to learn the ×9 multiplication facts. You'll need to use subtraction as you figure out these facts, so we're going to practice some subtraction first."

Write **40 – 6 =** on a piece of paper. "We'll use ten-frames to show this problem."

"How many tens do we need to show 40?" *Four.* Place four full ten-frames on the table.

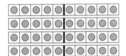

"Now, we need to subtract six from 40. We'll use a piece of paper to cover the six dots that we're subtracting." Slide a blank piece of paper from right to left over the bottom ten-frame until six dots are covered.

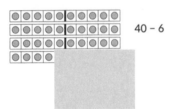
40 – 6

"How many dots are left showing?" *34.* If your child isn't sure, remind him to think about the number of tens and ones. There are three full ten-frames and four single dots, for a total of 34 dots. Tell your child that he can also use subtraction to help find the answer: since 10 – 6 = 4, there must be four dots left after six are covered.

$30 \begin{cases} \\ \\ \end{cases}$ 40 – 6 = 34

$10 – 6 = 4 \begin{cases} \end{cases}$

Have your child use the same process to solve the following problems. Each time, have him slide the blank paper to cover the number being subtracted, and encourage him to use subtraction facts to help find the answers.

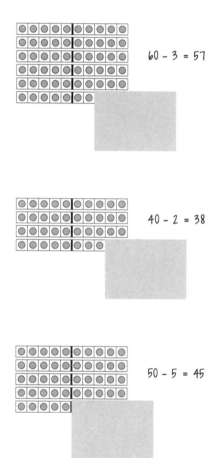

60 − 3 = 57

40 − 2 = 38

50 − 5 = 45

Note: This lesson is meant to be an introduction to mental subtraction, and it's not expected that your child will master it after just one practice session. He will become more skillful as he practices mental subtraction at the beginning of each lesson this week. Also, it's fine if your child is able to solve the problems without the ten-frames, or if he uses a different approach to finding the answers. What matters most is that he learns to quickly and confidently subtract a one-digit number from a multiple of ten (that is, a number like 30, 60, or 50).

Introduce ×9 facts

"This week, you're going to learn the ×9 multiplication facts. But you've actually already learned a lot of the ×9 facts!"

Make a list of the ×9 facts in order. (Do not include the answers.)

1 × 9 =
2 × 9 =
3 × 9 =
4 × 9 =
5 × 9 =
6 × 9 =
7 × 9 =
8 × 9 =
9 × 9 =
10 × 9 =

Have your child practice what he has learned in previous weeks to fill in the answers from 1 × 9 up to 6 × 9, as well as 10 × 9.

1 × 9 = 9
2 × 9 = 18
3 × 9 = 27
4 × 9 = 36
5 × 9 = 45
6 × 9 = 54
7 × 9 =
8 × 9 =
9 × 9 =
10 × 9 = 90

"There are only three ×9 facts left that you need to learn!"

Use ×10 facts to find ×9 facts

"You can use the ×10 facts and the commutative property to help you memorize the last three ×9 facts."

Write **10 × 7 =** on a piece of paper and slide the L-cover to match.

Have your child complete the written multiplication problem: **10 × 7 = 70.**

Write **9 × 7 =** directly *above* **10 × 7 = 70.** (Writing 9 × 7 *above* 10 × 7 makes the format consistent with the written times tables.)

"9 × 7 is just one group of seven less than 70. So, you can subtract seven from 70 to find the answer to 9 × 7." Slide the L-cover *up* to cover one more row of seven dots.

"So, what's 9 × 7?" *63.*

Have your child complete the written multiplication problem: **9 x 7 = 63.** Also have him use the commutative property to complete the related problem in the list of ×9 facts: **7 x 9 = 63.**

Repeat this activity with the remaining ×9 facts. Encourage your child to use the ×10 facts as stepping stones to the ×9 facts.

$$10 \times 8 = 80 \qquad 10 \times 9 = 90$$
$$9 \times 8 = 72 \qquad 9 \times 9 = 81$$

Play *Multiplication Race (×9)*

Play *Multiplication Race (×9)*. Use the same directions as in Week 1, but use the *Multiplication Race/Bump (×9)* game board (page 181) and multiply each card by nine, rather than by two.

Note: Save this game board for tomorrow's game as well.

Independent practice

Have your child complete Practice Pages 1A and 1B in the Week 7 section. On Practice Page 1B, remind your child to use each ×10 fact as a stepping stone to finding the answer to the ×9 fact below it. Answers are on page 315.

Day 2

Mental subtraction practice (if needed—see page 84)

Have your child use the ten-frames and a blank piece of paper to solve the following problems. Use the same process as in Day 1, and remind him to slide the blank piece of paper over the dots that are being subtracted.

$$60 - 5 = 55$$
$$80 - 2 = 78$$
$$40 - 7 = 33$$

Warm-up: Recite ×9 table

Have your child recite the ×9 table while sliding the L-cover to match each fact: *1 × 9 is 9. 2 × 9 is 18* . . .

Play *Multiplication Bump (×9)*

Play *Multiplication Bump (×9)*. Use the same directions as in Week 1, but use the *Multiplication Race/Bump (×9)* game board (page 181) and multiply each card by nine, rather than by two.

As you play, remind your child to use ×10 facts as stepping stones to finding the answer to the ×9 facts.

Independent practice

Have your child complete Practice Pages 2A and 2B in the Week 7 section. Answers are on page 315.

Day 3

Mental subtraction practice (if needed—see page 84)

Have your child use the ten-frames and a blank piece of paper to solve the following problems. Use the same process as in Day 1, and remind him to slide the blank piece of paper over the dots that are being subtracted.

80 – 4 = 76

70 – 6 = 64

30 – 9 = 21

Warm-up: Recite ×9 table

Have your child recite the ×9 table while sliding the L-cover to match each fact. *1 × 9 is 9. 2 × 9 is 18 . . .*

Play *Four in a Row (×9)*

Play *Four in a Row (×9)*. Use the same directions as in Week 1, but use the *Four in a Row (×9)* game board (page 183) and multiply each card by nine, rather than by two.

Independent practice

Have your child complete Practice Pages 3A and 3B in the Week 7 section. Answers are on page 316.

Day 4

Mental subtraction practice (if needed—see page 84)

Have your child use the ten-frames and a blank piece of paper to solve the following problems. Use the same process as in Day 1, and remind him to slide the blank piece of paper over the dots that are being subtracted.

60 - 3 = 57
50 - 8 = 42
40 - 7 = 33

Warm-up: Recite ×9 table

Have your child recite the ×9 tables. Encourage him to do so from memory, without using the dot array. However, if he has trouble, allow him to use the dot array and L-cover while reciting.

Play *Roll and Cover (×9)*

Play *Roll and Cover (×9)*. Use the same directions as in Week 1, but use the *Roll and Cover (×9)* game board (page 185) and multiply the total of the dice by nine, rather than by two. For example, if you roll a *1*, cover the *54* on the game board, since 1 + 5 = 6, and 6 × 9 = 54.

Independent practice

Have your child complete Practice Pages 4A and 4B in the Week 7 section. Answers are on page 316.

Day 5

Mental subtraction practice (if needed—see page 84)

Have your child use the ten-frames and a blank piece of paper to solve the following problems. Use the same process as in Day 1, and remind him to slide the blank piece of paper over the number of dots being subtracted.

90 – 9 = 81
80 – 8 = 72
70 – 7 = 63

Warm-up: Recite ×9 table

Have your child recite the ×9 table. If he has trouble recalling the facts from memory, allow him to use the L-cover and dot array while reciting.

Play *Over Under (×9)*

Play *Over Under (×9)*. Use the same directions as in Week 1, but use the *Over Under (×9)* game board (page 187) and multiply the number on the card by nine, rather than by two.

If the answer is less than 48, the player who is "Under" wins the card and places it in the "Under" box. If the answer is greater than 48, the player who is "Over" wins the card and places it in the "Over" box.

Independent practice

Have your child complete Practice Pages 5A and 5B in the Week 7 section. Answers are on page 317.

Once your child finishes the Practice Pages, point out that he has now learned 96 of the 100 facts in the multiplication chart on Practice Page 5A. In just a couple more weeks, he'll have all 100 mastered!

WEEK 8

x7 FACTS

WEEK 8 AT A GLANCE

Your child will memorize the ×7 facts this week. Since she's already learned most of the ×7 facts in previous weeks, she only has two more to learn: 7 × 7 and 7 × 8. Many children find these two facts the most difficult to memorize, so your child will practice these two facts intensively this week, along with reviewing the other ×7 facts.

This week, your child will learn these facts:

$1 \times 7 = 7$
$2 \times 7 = 14$
$3 \times 7 = 21$
$4 \times 7 = 28$
$5 \times 7 = 35$
$6 \times 7 = 42$
$7 \times 7 = 49$
$8 \times 7 = 56$
$9 \times 7 = 63$
$10 \times 7 = 70$

Day 1

Introduce ×7 facts

"This week, you're going to learn the ×7 multiplication facts. But you've actually already learned nearly all of them!"

Make a list of the ×7 facts in order. (Do not include the answers.)

1 × 7 =
2 × 7 =
3 × 7 =
4 × 7 =
5 × 7 =
6 × 7 =
7 × 7 =
8 × 7 =
9 × 7 =
10 × 7 =

Have your child use what she has learned in previous weeks to fill in the answers from 1 × 7 up to 6 × 7, as well as 9 ×7 and 10 × 7.

1 × 7 = 7
2 × 7 = 14
3 × 7 = 21
4 × 7 = 28
5 × 7 = 35
6 × 7 = 42
7 × 7 =
8 × 7 =
9 × 7 = 63
10 × 7 = 70

"There are only two ×7 facts that you still need to learn! You can use the ×7 facts you already know to help figure them out."

Slide the L-cover to match 6 × 7.

"7 × 7 is just one group of seven more than 42. So, you can add seven to 42 to find the answer to 7 × 7." Slide the L-cover down to show one more row of seven dots.

"So, what's 7 × 7?" *49.*

Have your child complete the written multiplication problem in the list of ×7 facts: **7 x 7 = 49.**

"8 × 7 is just one group of seven more than 49. So, you can add seven to 49 to find the answer to 8 × 7." Slide the L-cover down to show one more row of seven dots.

"So, what's 8 × 7?" *56.*

Have your child complete the written multiplication problem in the list of ×7 facts: **8 × 7 = 56**.

Play *Multiplication Race (×7)*

Play *Multiplication Race (×7).* Use the same directions as in Week 1, but use the *Multiplication Race/Bump (×7)* game board (page 165) and multiply each card by seven, rather than by two.

Note: Save this game board for tomorrow's game as well.

Independent practice

Have your child complete Practice Pages 1A and 1B in the Week 8 section. Answers are on page 317.

Day 2

Warm-up: Recite ×7 table

Have your child recite the ×7 table while sliding the L-cover to match each fact: *1 × 7 is 7. 2 × 7 is 14 . . .*

Play *Multiplication Bump (×7)*

Play *Multiplication Bump (×7).* Use the same directions as in Week 1, but use the *Multiplication Race/Bump (×7)* game board (page 165) and multiply each card by seven, rather than by two.

Independent practice

Have your child complete Practice Pages 2A and 2B in the Week 8 section. Answers are on page 318.

Day 3

Warm-up: Recite ×7 table

Have your child recite the ×7 table while sliding the L-cover to match each fact. *1 × 7 is 7. 2 × 7 is 14 . . .*

Play *Four in a Row (×7)*

Play *Four in a Row (×7).* Use the same directions as in Week 1, but use the *Four in a Row (×7)* game board (page 167) and multiply each card by seven, rather than by two.

Independent practice

Have your child complete Practice Pages 3A and 3B in the Week 8 section. Answers are on page 318.

Day 4

Warm-up: Recite ×7 table

Have your child recite the ×7 table. Encourage her to do so from memory, without using the dot array. However, if she has trouble, allow her to use the dot array and L-cover while reciting.

Play *Roll and Cover (×7)*

Play *Roll and Cover (×7)*. Use the same directions as in Week 1, but use the *Roll and Cover (×7)* game board (page 169) and multiply the total of the dice by seven, rather than by two. For example, if you roll a **4**, cover the **63** on the game board, since $4 + 5 = 9$, and $9 \times 7 = 63$.

Independent practice

Have your child complete Practice Pages 4A and 4B in the Week 8 section. Answers are on page 319.

Day 5

Warm-up: Recite ×7 table

Have your child recite the ×7 table. If she has trouble recalling the facts from memory, allow her to use the L-cover and dot array while reciting.

Play *Over Under (×7)*

Play *Over Under (×7)*. Use the same directions as in Week 1, but use the *Over Under (×7)* game board (page 171) and multiply the number on the card by seven, rather than by two.

If the answer is less than 40, the player who is "Under" wins the card and places it in the "Under" box. If the answer is greater than 40, the player who is "Over" wins the card and places it in the "Over" box.

Independent practice

Have your child complete Practice Pages 5A and 5B in the Week 8 section. Answers are on page 319.

Once your child finishes the Practice Pages, point out that she has now learned 99 of the 100 facts in the multiplication chart on Practice Page 5A. Only one multiplication fact to go!

WEEK 9

x8 FACTS

WEEK 9 AT A GLANCE

Your child only has one more multiplication fact to learn! This week, he'll learn 8 × 8 and review the rest of the ×8 facts.

This week, your child will learn these facts:

$1 \times 8 = 8$
$2 \times 8 = 16$
$3 \times 8 = 24$
$4 \times 8 = 32$
$5 \times 8 = 40$
$6 \times 8 = 48$
$7 \times 8 = 56$
$8 \times 8 = 64$
$9 \times 8 = 72$
$10 \times 8 = 80$

Day 1

Introduce ×8 facts

"This week, you're going to learn the ×8 multiplication facts. But you've already learned all of them except for one!"

Make a list of the ×8 facts in order as in previous weeks. (Do not include the answers.)

1 × 8 =
2 × 8 =
3 × 8 =
4 × 8 =
5 × 8 =
6 × 8 =
7 × 8 =
8 × 8 =
9 × 8 =
10 × 8 =

Have your child use what he has learned in previous weeks to fill in the answers for all of them except 8 × 8.

1 × 8 = 8
2 × 8 = 16
3 × 8 = 24
4 × 8 = 32
5 × 8 = 40
6 × 8 = 48
7 × 8 = 56
8 × 8 =
9 × 8 = 72
10 × 8 = 80

"You only need to learn one last ×8 fact. You can use 4 × 8 to help you memorize it."

Write **4 × 8 =** on a piece of paper and slide the L-cover to match.

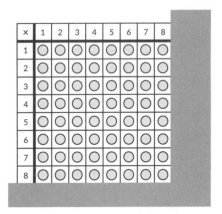

Have your child complete the written multiplication problem: **4 × 8 = 32.**

Write **8 × 8 =** below **4 × 8 = 32.**

"8 × 8 is twice as many groups of eight as 4 × 8. So, you can double 32 to find the answer to 8 × 8." Slide the L-cover down to show four more rows of eight dots.

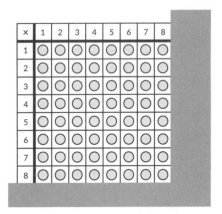

"So, what's 8 × 8?" *64.*

Have your child complete the written multiplication problem in the list of ×8 facts: **8 x 8 = 64.**

Play *Multiplication Race (×8)*

Play *Multiplication Race (×8)*. Use the same directions as in Week 1, but use the *Multiplication Race/Bump (×8)* game board (page 173) and multiply each card by eight, rather than by two.

Note: Save this game board for tomorrow's game as well.

Independent practice

Have your child complete Practice Pages 1A and 1B in the Week 9 section. Answers are on page 320.

Day 2

Warm-up: Recite ×8 table

Have your child recite the ×8 table while sliding the L-cover to match each fact: *1 × 8 is 8. 2 × 8 is 16 . . .*

Play *Multiplication Bump (×8)*

Play *Multiplication Bump (×8)*. Use the same directions as in Week 1, but use the *Multiplication Race/Bump (×8)* game board (page 173) and multiply each card by eight, rather than by two.

Independent practice

Have your child complete Practice Pages 2A and 2B in the Week 9 section. Answers are on page 320.

Day 3

Warm-up: Recite ×8 table

Have your child recite the ×8 table while sliding the L-cover to match each fact. *1 × 8 is 8. 2 × 8 is 16 . . .*

Play *Four in a Row (×8)*

Play *Four in a Row (×8)*. Use the same directions as in Week 1, but use the *Four in a Row (×8)* game board (page 175) and multiply each card by eight, rather than by two.

Independent practice

Have your child complete Practice Pages 3A and 3B of the Week 9 section. Answers are on page 321.

Day 4

Warm-up: Recite ×8 table

Have your child recite the ×8 table. Encourage him to do so from memory, without using the dot array. However, if he has trouble, allow him to use the dot array and L-cover while reciting.

Play *Roll and Cover (×8)*

Play *Roll and Cover (×8)*. Use the same directions as in Week 1, but use the *Roll and Cover (×8)* game board (page 177) and multiply the total of the dice by eight, rather than by two. For example, if you roll a *2*, cover the *56* on the game board, since 2 + 5 = 7, and 7 × 8 = 56.

Independent practice

Have your child complete Practice Pages 4A and 4B in the Week 9 section. Answers are on page 321.

Day 5

Warm-up: Recite ×8 table

Have your child recite the ×8 table. If he has trouble recalling the facts from memory, allow him to use the L-cover and dot array while reciting.

Play *Over Under (×8)*

Play *Over Under (×8)*. Use the same directions as in Week 1, but use the *Over Under (×8)* game board (page 179) and multiply the number on the card by eight, rather than by two.

If the answer is less than 45, the player who is "Under" wins the card and places it in the "Under" box. If the answer is greater than 45, the player who is "Over" wins the card and places it in the "Over" box.

Independent practice

Have your child complete Practice Pages 5A and 5B in the Week 9 section. Answers are on page 322.

Once your child finishes the Practice Pages, point out that he has now learned all 100 of the 100 facts in the multiplication chart on Practice Page 5A! Next week, he'll review and practice the facts to make sure they are all thoroughly learned.

WEEK 10

REVIEW

WEEK 10 AT A GLANCE

Congratulations—your child has learned all of the multiplication facts!

In this final week, your child will play a new game and complete Practice Pages that review and practice all of the multiplication facts (along with a little extra practice of the most-frequently-forgotten facts, like 8×6 and 7×7). This final week of practice will help cement the multiplication facts in your child's head so that they truly stick.

Day 1

Warm-up: Recite ×8 table

Have your child recite the ×8 table from memory.

Play *Multiplication War*

Teach your child how to play *Multiplication War* and play one time.

MATERIALS

* Deck of cards, with face cards removed (40 cards total)

OBJECT OF THE GAME

Win the most cards.

HOW TO PLAY

As in the regular card game War, shuffle the cards and deal out an equal number of cards to each player. Players place their cards face down in a pile.

To play, turn over the top two cards in your pile and multiply their numbers together. For example, if you turn over a *5* and a *7*, say, "5 × 7 equals 35." Then the other player does the same. Whoever's answer is greater wins all four cards. If the answers are equal, play again. The player whose answer is greater wins all eight cards. Set aside the cards that are won.

Play until both players use up all the cards in their piles. Whoever wins the most cards wins the game.

Independent practice

Have your child complete Practice Pages 1A and 1B in the Week 10 section. Answers are on page 322.

Day 2

Warm-up: Recite ×7 table

Have your child recite the ×7 table from memory.

Play *Multiplication War*

Play *Multiplication War*. (See Day 1 for directions.)

Independent practice

Have your child complete Practice Pages 2A and 2B in the Week 10 section. Answers are on page 323.

Day 3

Warm-up: Recite ×9 table

Have your child recite the ×9 table from memory.

Play *Multiplication War*

Play *Multiplication War*. (See Day 1 for directions.)

Independent practice

Have your child complete Practice Pages 3A and 3B in the Week 10 section. Answers are on page 323.

Day 4

Warm-up: Recite ×7 table

Have your child recite the ×7 table. Encourage her to do so from memory, without using the dot array. However, if she has trouble, allow her to use the dot array and L-cover while reciting.

Play *Multiplication War*

Play *Multiplication War*. (See Day 1 for directions.)

Independent practice

Have your child complete Practice Pages 4A and 4B in the Week 10 section. Answers are on page 324.

Day 5

Warm-up: Recite ×8 table

Have your child recite the ×8 table. If she has trouble recalling the facts from memory, allow her to use the L-cover and dot array while reciting.

Play *Multiplication War*

Play *Multiplication War*. (See Day 1 for directions.)

Independent practice

Have your child complete Practice Pages 5A and 5B in the Week 10 section. Answers are on page 324.

Congratulations!

Your child has now learned all 100 multiplication facts from 1 × 1 to 10 × 10!

I hope you and your child have enjoyed the games and activities, and that you'll take some time to celebrate your child's accomplishment (and your own hard work, too)!

If your child still struggles to recall some of the multiplication facts automatically, continue playing the games and encouraging your child to use stepping-stone facts to help figure out the answers. Some children simply need a little more practice before they know all the facts with ease. The multiplication facts are essential building blocks for higher-level topics like division, fractions, ratios, proportions, and algebra, so don't be afraid to spend as long as you need until the multiplication facts really stick for your child.

GAME BOARDS

Dot Array

×	1	2	3	4	5	6	7	8	9	10
1	●	●	●	●	●	●	●	●	●	●
2	●	●	●	●	●	●	●	●	●	●
3	●	●	●	●	●	●	●	●	●	●
4	●	●	●	●	●	●	●	●	●	●
5	●	●	●	●	●	●	●	●	●	●
6	●	●	●	●	●	●	●	●	●	●
7	●	●	●	●	●	●	●	●	●	●
8	●	●	●	●	●	●	●	●	●	●
9	●	●	●	●	●	●	●	●	●	●
10	●	●	●	●	●	●	●	●	●	●

L-Cover

Cut on the dotted line and remove this section. (You will be left with a gray L.)

Ten-Frames

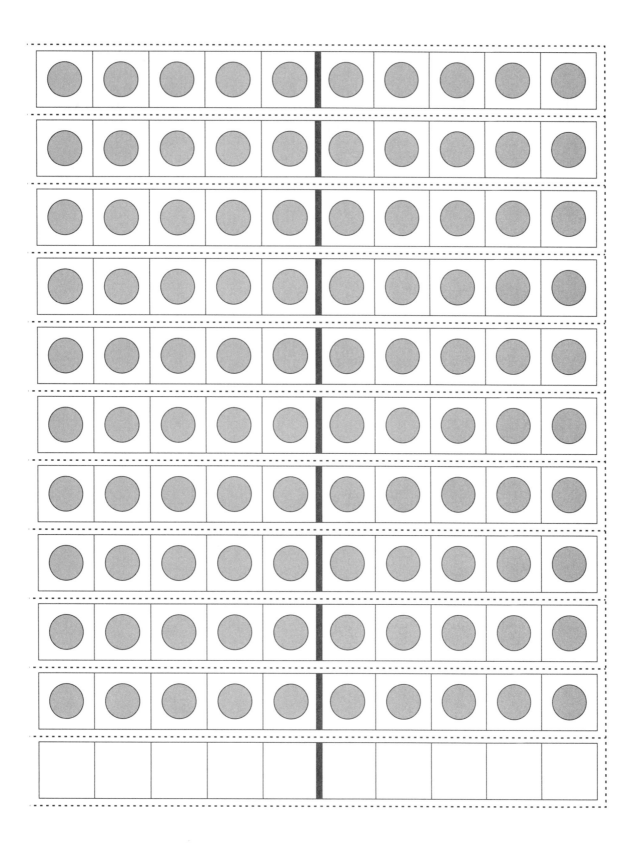

Multiplication Race/Bump (×2) Game Board

2	4	6	8	10	12	14	16	18	20

Four in a Row (×2) Game Board

8	14	20	18	6	4
2	12	10	16	2	18
10	4	6	12	20	14
16	8	14	20	18	6
12	16	2	8	10	20
6	10	18	14	12	2

Roll and Cover (×2) Game Board

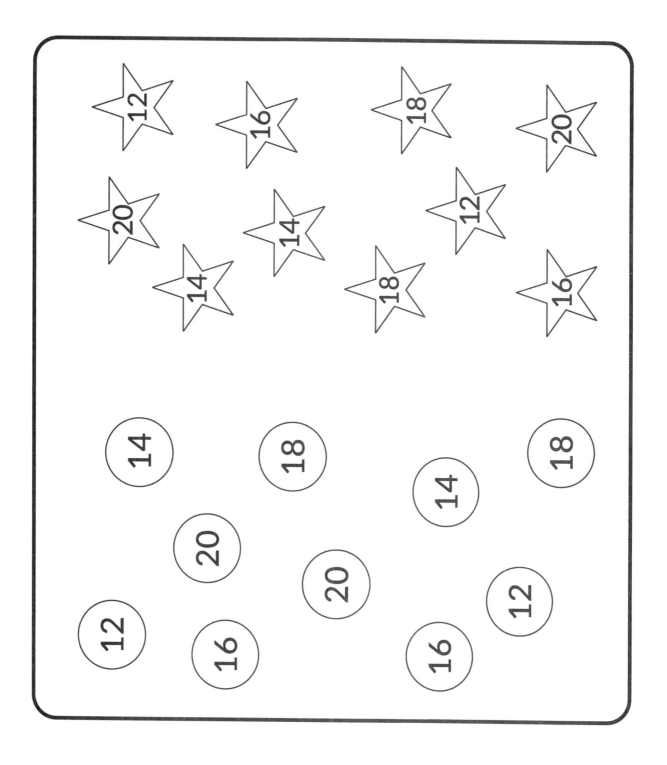

Over Under (×2) Game Board

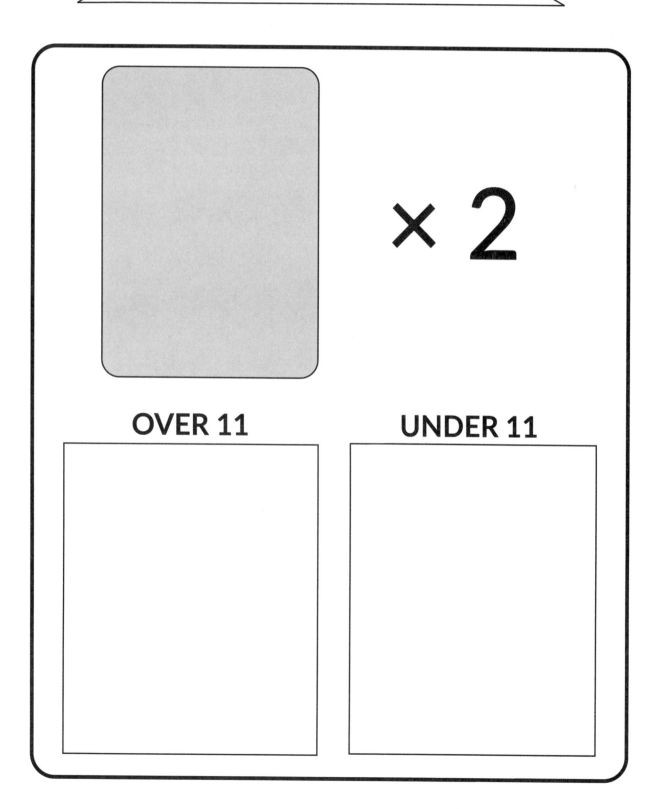

× 2

OVER 11   **UNDER 11**

Multiplication Race/Bump (×3) Game Board

| 3 | 6 | 9 | 12 | 15 | 18 | 21 | 24 | 27 | 30 |

Four in a Row (×3) Game Board

24	3	21	15	27	12
18	30	9	6	21	24
12	6	27	9	30	18
15	12	3	18	24	9
6	27	15	21	3	30
3	18	12	30	9	27

Roll and Cover (×3) Game Board

Over Under (×3) Game Board

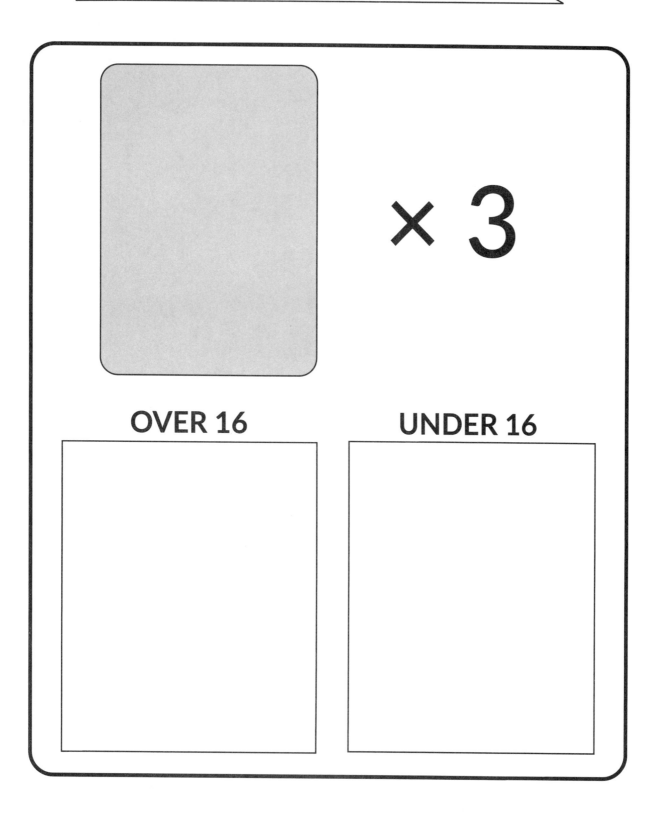

OVER 16

UNDER 16

Multiplication Race/Bump (×4) Game Board

4	8	12	16	20	24	28	32	36	40

Four in a Row (×4) Game Board

32	40	4	28	36	8
24	12	20	16	4	40
16	36	32	8	20	12
20	32	24	12	28	36
4	24	40	32	16	28
32	28	12	20	8	16

Roll and Cover (×4) Game Board

Over Under (×4) Game Board

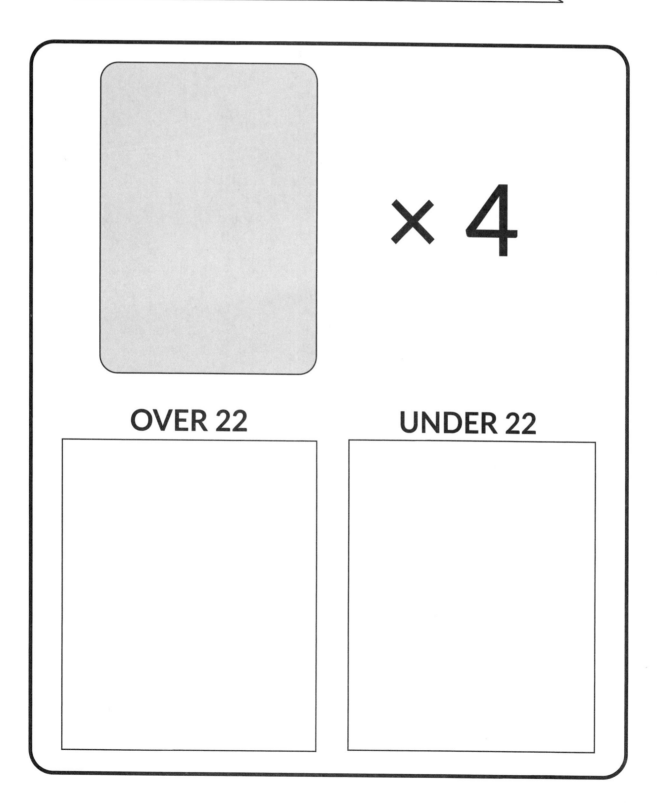

× 4

OVER 22

UNDER 22

Multiplication Race/Bump (×5) Game Board

5	10	15	20	25	30	35	40	45	50

Four in a Row (×5) Game Board

30	25	45	5	50	20
10	40	15	35	5	45
20	15	40	50	30	25
35	10	30	40	25	15
45	20	50	10	40	50
15	35	25	45	20	30

Roll and Cover (×5) Game Board

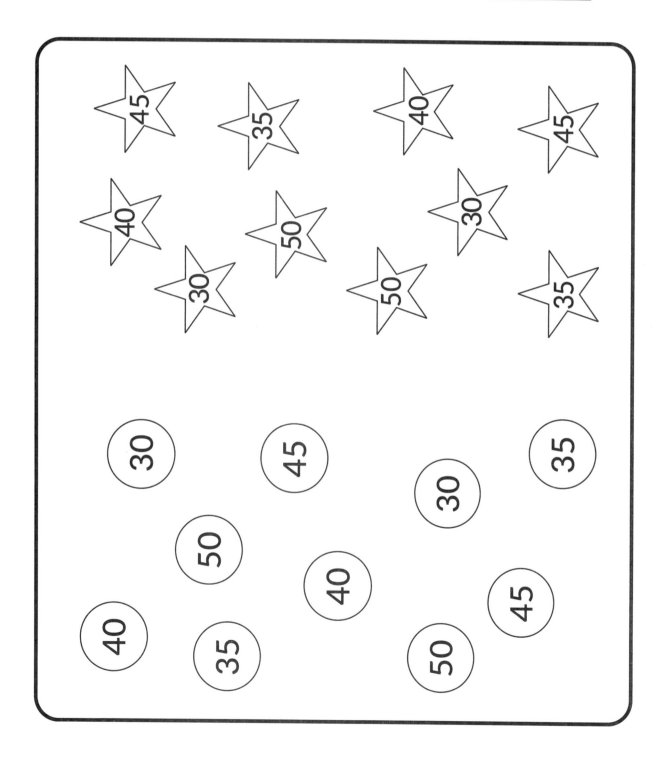

Over Under (×5) Game Board

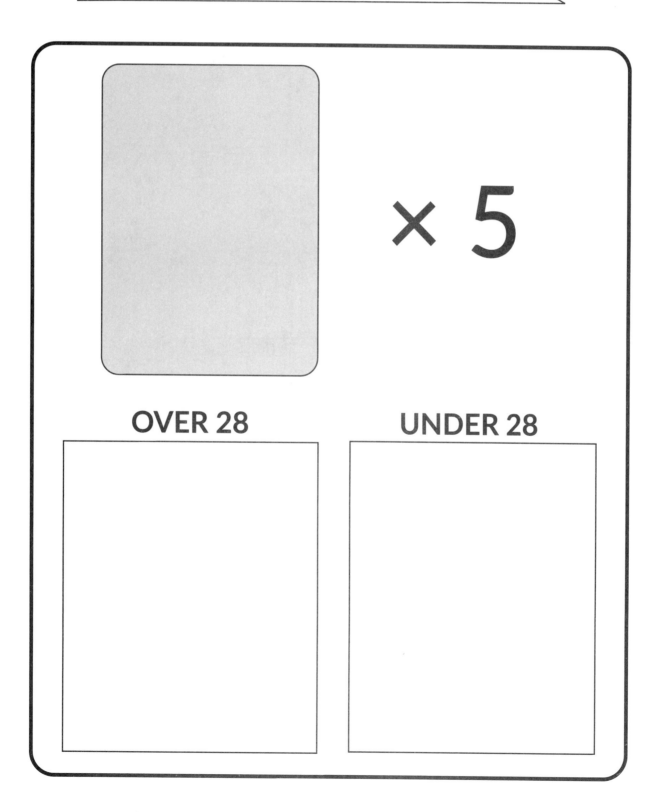

× 5

OVER 28

UNDER 28

Multiplication Race/Bump (×6) Game Board

6	12	18	24	30	36	42	48	54	60

Four in a Row (×6) Game Board

48	30	54	24	60	6
54	18	30	42	12	36
6	24	48	36	18	12
12	42	60	54	36	24
42	48	6	18	30	60
30	12	24	6	54	48

Roll and Cover (×6) Game Board

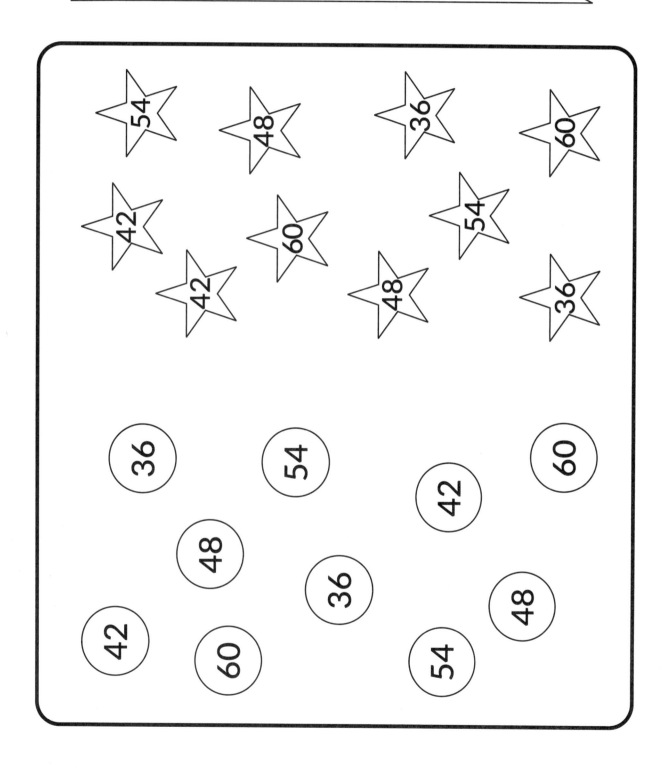

Over Under (×6) Game Board

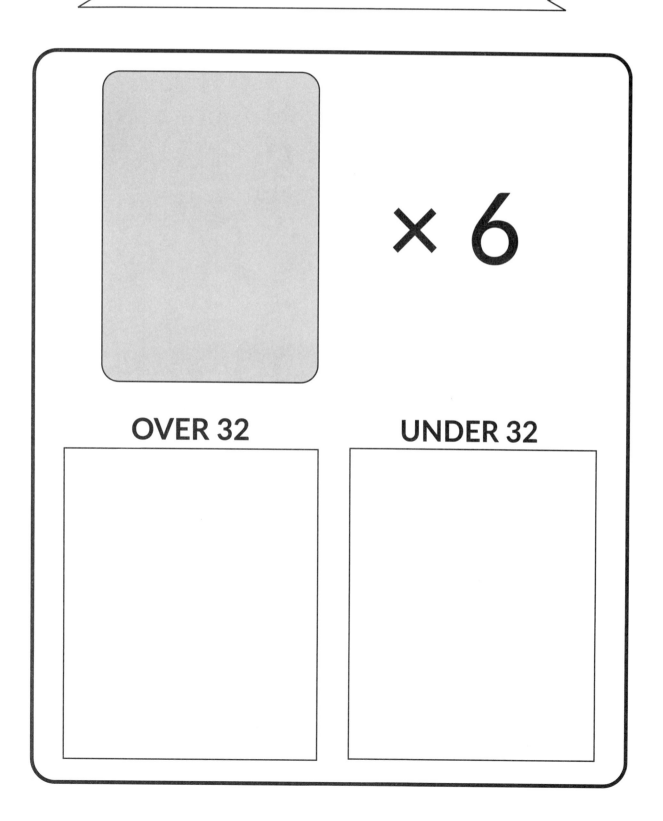

Multiplication Race/Bump (×7) Game Board

7	14	21	28	35	42	49	56	63	70

Four in a Row (×7) Game Board

70	42	14	63	7	49
7	35	21	56	70	28
49	63	28	14	21	42
42	28	56	49	35	14
35	7	63	21	56	70
56	14	7	42	63	35

Roll and Cover (×7) Game Board

Stars: 63, 42, 70, 56, 49, 56, 49, 70, 42, 63

Circles: 49, 56, 56, 42, 42, 70, 63, 70, 63, 49

Over Under (×7) Game Board

× 7

OVER 40

UNDER 40

Multiplication Race/Bump (×8) Game Board

8	16	24	32	40	48	56	64	72	80

Four in a Row (×8) Game Board

24	8	48	40	72	80
16	64	80	56	32	40
32	48	16	24	64	8
8	40	72	56	16	24
64	80	32	48	56	72
72	16	56	8	40	32

Roll and Cover (×8) Game Board

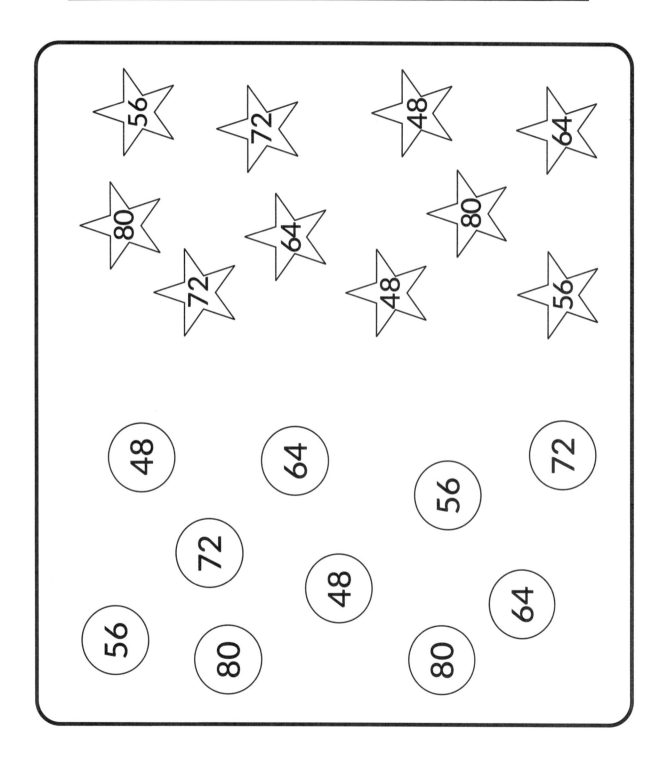

Over Under (×8) Game Board

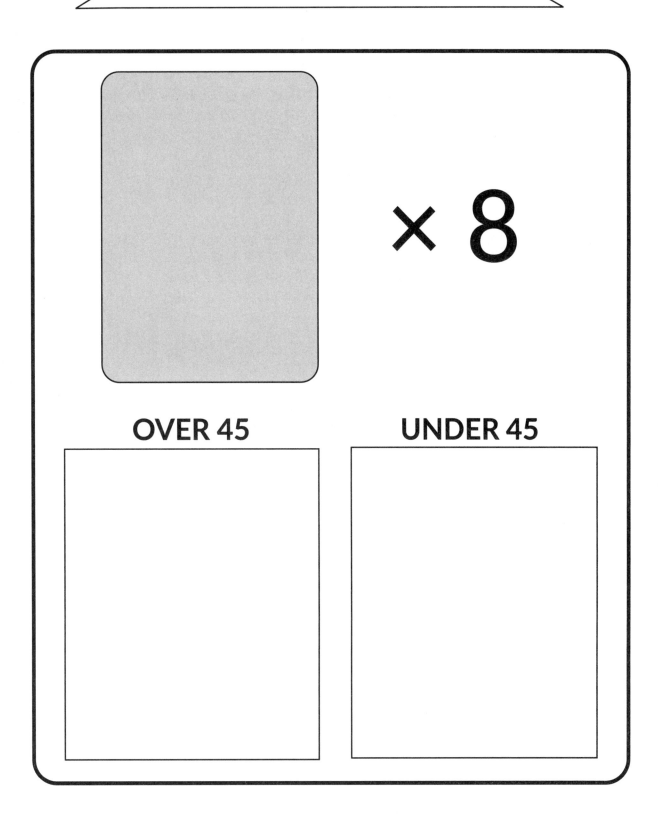

× 8

OVER 45

UNDER 45

Multiplication Race/Bump (×9) Game Board

9	18	27	36	45	54	63	72	81	90

Four in a Row (×9) Game Board

54	9	72	36	81	45
18	63	27	90	36	9
90	45	81	63	18	27
63	54	9	72	72	90
81	27	18	45	54	36
27	81	36	54	9	18

Roll and Cover (×9) Game Board

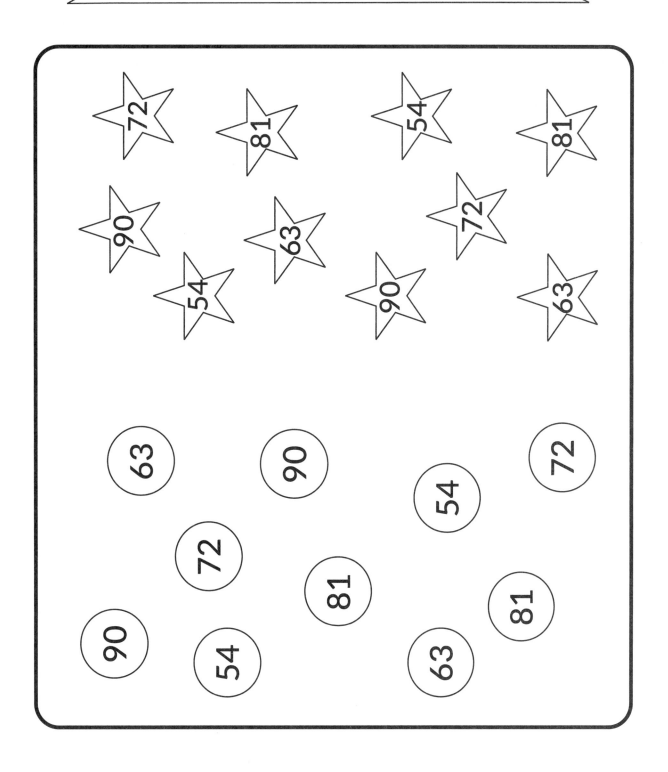

Over Under (×9) Game Board

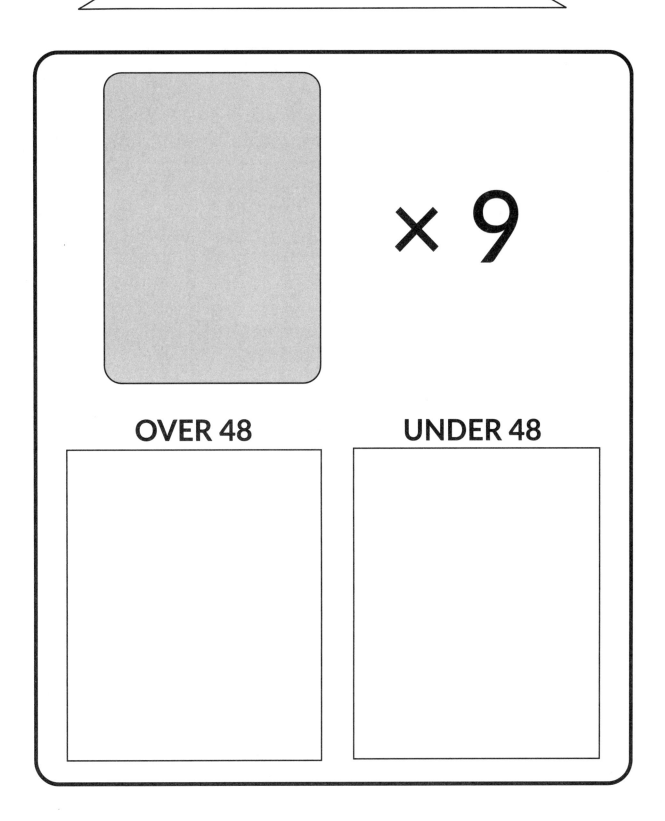

× 9

OVER 48

UNDER 48

Multiplication Race/Bump (×10) Game Board

| 10 | 20 | 30 | 40 | 50 | 60 | 70 | 80 | 90 | 100 |

Four in a Row (×10) Game Board

40	60	10	100	80	70
100	20	30	90	50	10
80	50	60	30	70	90
60	90	100	20	40	50
20	10	40	70	30	80
90	30	20	50	100	40

Roll and Cover (×10) Game Board

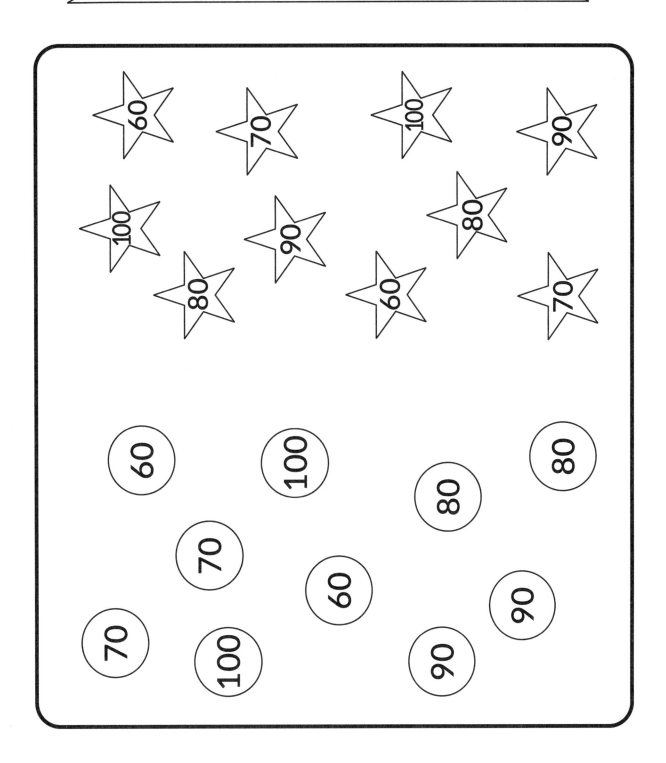

Over Under (×10) Game Board

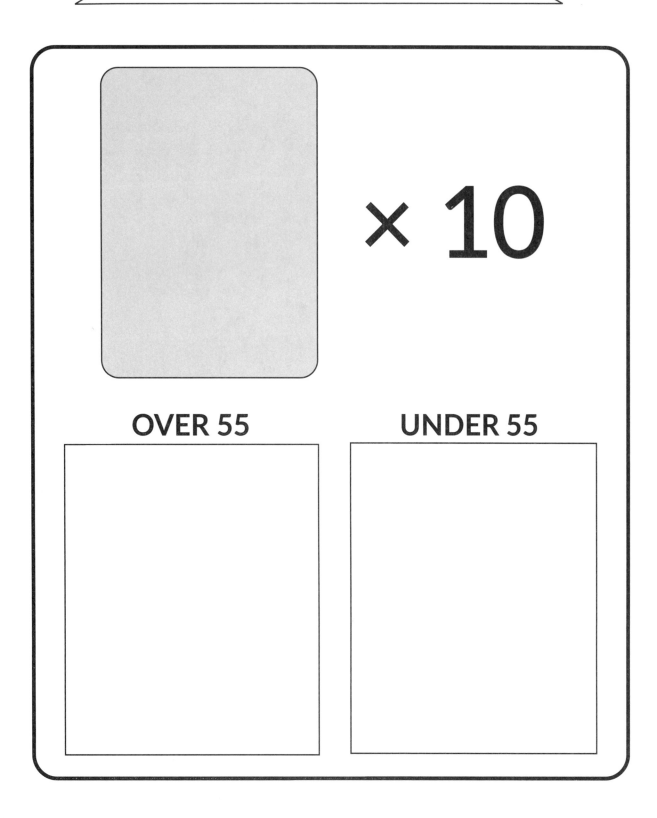

× 10

OVER 55

UNDER 55

PRACTICE PAGES

| Week 1 | Practice Page 1A |

$1 \times 2 =$ _____ ● ●

$2 \times 2 =$ _____ ● ●

$3 \times 2 =$ _____ ● ●

$4 \times 2 =$ _____ ● ●

$5 \times 2 =$ _____ ● ●

$6 \times 2 =$ _____ ● ●

$7 \times 2 =$ _____ ● ●

$8 \times 2 =$ _____ ● ●

$9 \times 2 =$ _____ ● ●

$10 \times 2 =$ _____ ● ●

Week 1	Practice Page 1B

$3 \times 2 =$ _____ $2 \times 2 =$ _____ $4 \times 2 =$ _____

$5 \times 2 =$ _____ $6 \times 2 =$ _____ $8 \times 2 =$ _____

$10 \times 2 =$ _____ $7 \times 2 =$ _____ $9 \times 2 =$ _____

Week 1	Practice Page 2A

1 × 2 = _____

2 × 2 = _____

3 × 2 = _____

4 × 2 = _____

5 × 2 = _____

6 × 2 = _____

7 × 2 = _____

8 × 2 = _____

9 × 2 = _____

10 × 2 = _____

| Week 1 | Practice Page 2B |

$4 \times 2 =$ _____ $2 \times 2 =$ _____ $3 \times 2 =$ _____

$7 \times 2 =$ _____ $6 \times 2 =$ _____ $5 \times 2 =$ _____

$9 \times 2 =$ _____ $8 \times 2 =$ _____ $10 \times 2 =$ _____

Week 1	Practice Page 3A

$1 \times 2 =$ ____

$2 \times 2 =$ ____

$3 \times 2 =$ ____

$4 \times 2 =$ ____

$5 \times 2 =$ ____

$6 \times 2 =$ ____

$7 \times 2 =$ ____

$8 \times 2 =$ ____

$9 \times 2 =$ ____

$10 \times 2 =$ ____

Week 1	Practice Page 3B

$6 \times 2 =$ _____ $9 \times 2 =$ _____ $8 \times 2 =$ _____

$5 \times 2 =$ _____ $10 \times 2 =$ _____ $2 \times 2 =$ _____

$4 \times 2 =$ _____ $7 \times 2 =$ _____ $3 \times 2 =$ _____

$2 \times 7 =$ _____ $2 \times 2 =$ _____ $2 \times 8 =$ _____

$2 \times 10 =$ _____ $2 \times 9 =$ _____ $2 \times 3 =$ _____

$2 \times 6 =$ _____ $2 \times 4 =$ _____ $2 \times 5 =$ _____

| Week 1 | Practice Page 4A |

$1 \times 1 =$ _____ $1 \times 2 =$ _____

$2 \times 1 =$ _____ $2 \times 2 =$ _____

$3 \times 1 =$ _____ $3 \times 2 =$ _____

$4 \times 1 =$ _____ $4 \times 2 =$ _____

$5 \times 1 =$ _____ $5 \times 2 =$ _____

$6 \times 1 =$ _____ $6 \times 2 =$ _____

$7 \times 1 =$ _____ $7 \times 2 =$ _____

$8 \times 1 =$ _____ $8 \times 2 =$ _____

$9 \times 1 =$ _____ $9 \times 2 =$ _____

$10 \times 1 =$ _____ $10 \times 2 =$ _____

Week 1	Practice Page 4B

$8 \times 1 =$ _____ $10 \times 1 =$ _____ $9 \times 1 =$ _____

$2 \times 1 =$ _____ $6 \times 1 =$ _____ $5 \times 1 =$ _____

$10 \times 2 =$ _____ $7 \times 1 =$ _____ $4 \times 2 =$ _____

$9 \times 2 =$ _____ $8 \times 2 =$ _____ $7 \times 2 =$ _____

$3 \times 2 =$ _____ $3 \times 1 =$ _____ $4 \times 1 =$ _____

$2 \times 2 =$ _____ $1 \times 1 =$ _____ $6 \times 2 =$ _____

Week 1	Practice Page 5A

×	1	2	3	4	5	6	7	8	9	10
1										
2										
3										
4										
5										
6										
7										
8										
9										
10										

| Week 1 | Practice Page 5B |

$$
\begin{array}{ccccc}
1 & 6 & 9 & 2 & 10 \\
\times\ 2 & \times\ 2 & \times\ 2 & \times\ 2 & \times\ 2 \\
\hline
\end{array}
$$

$$
\begin{array}{ccccc}
3 & 4 & 8 & 5 & 7 \\
\times\ 2 & \times\ 2 & \times\ 2 & \times\ 2 & \times\ 2 \\
\hline
\end{array}
$$

$$
\begin{array}{ccccc}
8 & 2 & 4 & 5 & 9 \\
\times\ 1 & \times\ 1 & \times\ 1 & \times\ 1 & \times\ 1 \\
\hline
\end{array}
$$

$$
\begin{array}{ccccc}
10 & 3 & 7 & 1 & 6 \\
\times\ 1 & \times\ 1 & \times\ 1 & \times\ 1 & \times\ 1 \\
\hline
\end{array}
$$

Week 2	Practice Page 1A

$1 \times 3 = \underline{\hspace{1.5em}}$ $1 \times 2 = \underline{\hspace{1.5em}}$

$2 \times 3 = \underline{\hspace{1.5em}}$ $2 \times 2 = \underline{\hspace{1.5em}}$

$3 \times 3 = \underline{\hspace{1.5em}}$ $3 \times 2 = \underline{\hspace{1.5em}}$

$4 \times 3 = \underline{\hspace{1.5em}}$ $4 \times 2 = \underline{\hspace{1.5em}}$

$5 \times 3 = \underline{\hspace{1.5em}}$ $5 \times 2 = \underline{\hspace{1.5em}}$

$6 \times 3 = \underline{\hspace{1.5em}}$ $6 \times 2 = \underline{\hspace{1.5em}}$

$7 \times 3 = \underline{\hspace{1.5em}}$ $7 \times 2 = \underline{\hspace{1.5em}}$

$8 \times 3 = \underline{\hspace{1.5em}}$ $8 \times 2 = \underline{\hspace{1.5em}}$

$9 \times 3 = \underline{\hspace{1.5em}}$ $9 \times 2 = \underline{\hspace{1.5em}}$

$10 \times 3 = \underline{\hspace{1.5em}}$ $10 \times 2 = \underline{\hspace{1.5em}}$

Week 2		Practice Page 1B

2 × 1 = _____ 3 × 1 = _____	2 × 2 = _____ 3 × 2 = _____	2 × 3 = _____ 3 × 3 = ____
2 × 4 = _____ 3 × 4 = ____	2 × 5 = _____ 3 × 5 = _____	2 × 6 = _____ 3 × 6 = ____
2 × 7 = _____ 3 × 7 = _____	2 × 8 = _____ 3 × 8 = _____	2 × 9 = _____ 3 × 9 = _____
2 × 10 = _____ 3 × 10 = _____		

| Week 2 | Practice Page 2A |

1 × 3 = _____   1 × 1 = _____

2 × 3 = _____   2 × 1 = _____

3 × 3 = _____   3 × 1 = _____

4 × 3 = _____   4 × 1 = _____

5 × 3 = _____   5 × 1 = _____

6 × 3 = _____   6 × 1 = _____

7 × 3 = _____   7 × 1 = _____

8 × 3 = _____   8 × 1 = _____

9 × 3 = _____   9 × 1 = _____

10 × 3 = _____   10 × 1 = _____

| Week 2 | Practice Page 2B |

$2 \times 3 =$ _____ $8 \times 3 =$ _____ $3 \times 3 =$ _____

$4 \times 3 =$ _____ $5 \times 3 =$ _____ $1 \times 3 =$ _____

$9 \times 3 =$ _____ $7 \times 3 =$ _____ $10 \times 3 =$ _____

$6 \times 3 =$ _____ $1 \times 7 =$ _____ $2 \times 8 =$ _____

$1 \times 9 =$ _____ $10 \times 2 =$ _____ $4 \times 1 =$ _____

$2 \times 7 =$ _____ $2 \times 1 =$ _____ $9 \times 1 =$ _____

$5 \times 1 =$ _____ $9 \times 2 =$ _____ $3 \times 2 =$ _____

$10 \times 1 =$ _____ $6 \times 1 =$ _____ $6 \times 2 =$ _____

$2 \times 5 =$ _____ $4 \times 2 =$ _____ $2 \times 10 =$ _____

Week 2	Practice Page 3A

$1 \times 3 = \underline{\hspace{1cm}}$ $1 \times 2 = \underline{\hspace{1cm}}$

$2 \times 3 = \underline{\hspace{1cm}}$ $2 \times 2 = \underline{\hspace{1cm}}$

$3 \times 3 = \underline{\hspace{1cm}}$ $3 \times 2 = \underline{\hspace{1cm}}$

$4 \times 3 = \underline{\hspace{1cm}}$ $4 \times 2 = \underline{\hspace{1cm}}$

$5 \times 3 = \underline{\hspace{1cm}}$ $5 \times 2 = \underline{\hspace{1cm}}$

$6 \times 3 = \underline{\hspace{1cm}}$ $6 \times 2 = \underline{\hspace{1cm}}$

$7 \times 3 = \underline{\hspace{1cm}}$ $7 \times 2 = \underline{\hspace{1cm}}$

$8 \times 3 = \underline{\hspace{1cm}}$ $8 \times 2 = \underline{\hspace{1cm}}$

$9 \times 3 = \underline{\hspace{1cm}}$ $9 \times 2 = \underline{\hspace{1cm}}$

$10 \times 3 = \underline{\hspace{1cm}}$ $10 \times 2 = \underline{\hspace{1cm}}$

Week 2	Practice Page 3B

$$\begin{array}{r} 1 \\ \times\ 3 \\ \hline \end{array} \qquad \begin{array}{r} 6 \\ \times\ 3 \\ \hline \end{array} \qquad \begin{array}{r} 9 \\ \times\ 3 \\ \hline \end{array} \qquad \begin{array}{r} 2 \\ \times\ 3 \\ \hline \end{array} \qquad \begin{array}{r} 10 \\ \times\ 3 \\ \hline \end{array}$$

$$\begin{array}{r} 3 \\ \times\ 3 \\ \hline \end{array} \qquad \begin{array}{r} 4 \\ \times\ 3 \\ \hline \end{array} \qquad \begin{array}{r} 8 \\ \times\ 3 \\ \hline \end{array} \qquad \begin{array}{r} 5 \\ \times\ 3 \\ \hline \end{array} \qquad \begin{array}{r} 7 \\ \times\ 3 \\ \hline \end{array}$$

$$\begin{array}{r} 8 \\ \times\ 2 \\ \hline \end{array} \qquad \begin{array}{r} 2 \\ \times\ 2 \\ \hline \end{array} \qquad \begin{array}{r} 4 \\ \times\ 1 \\ \hline \end{array} \qquad \begin{array}{r} 4 \\ \times\ 2 \\ \hline \end{array} \qquad \begin{array}{r} 9 \\ \times\ 2 \\ \hline \end{array}$$

$$\begin{array}{r} 10 \\ \times\ 1 \\ \hline \end{array} \qquad \begin{array}{r} 2 \\ \times\ 9 \\ \hline \end{array} \qquad \begin{array}{r} 7 \\ \times\ 2 \\ \hline \end{array} \qquad \begin{array}{r} 1 \\ \times\ 9 \\ \hline \end{array} \qquad \begin{array}{r} 2 \\ \times\ 6 \\ \hline \end{array}$$

$$\begin{array}{r} 8 \\ \times\ 1 \\ \hline \end{array} \qquad \begin{array}{r} 5 \\ \times\ 2 \\ \hline \end{array} \qquad \begin{array}{r} 3 \\ \times\ 2 \\ \hline \end{array} \qquad \begin{array}{r} 1 \\ \times\ 5 \\ \hline \end{array} \qquad \begin{array}{r} 2 \\ \times\ 10 \\ \hline \end{array}$$

Week 2	Practice Page 4A

$1 \times 3 = $ _____ $1 \times 1 = $ _____

$2 \times 3 = $ _____ $2 \times 1 = $ _____

$3 \times 3 = $ _____ $3 \times 1 = $ _____

$4 \times 3 = $ _____ $4 \times 1 = $ _____

$5 \times 3 = $ _____ $5 \times 1 = $ _____

$6 \times 3 = $ _____ $6 \times 1 = $ _____

$7 \times 3 = $ _____ $7 \times 1 = $ _____

$8 \times 3 = $ _____ $8 \times 1 = $ _____

$9 \times 3 = $ _____ $9 \times 1 = $ _____

$10 \times 3 = $ _____ $10 \times 1 = $ _____

| Week 2 | Practice Page 4B |

1 × 3 = _____   3 × 8 = _____   2 × 2 = _____

4 × 2 = _____   3 × 1 = _____   8 × 1 = _____

5 × 1 = _____   6 × 2 = _____   3 × 3 = _____

3 × 7 = _____   1 × 7 = _____   2 × 8 = _____

1 × 9 = _____   10 × 3 = _____   4 × 1 = _____

2 × 7 = _____   2 × 3 = _____   9 × 3 = _____

5 × 3 = _____   9 × 2 = _____   3 × 2 = _____

10 × 1 = _____   6 × 1 = _____   6 × 3 = _____

2 × 5 = _____   4 × 3 = _____   2 × 10 = _____

Week 2   **Practice Page 5A**

×	1	2	3	4	5	6	7	8	9	10
1										
2										
3										
4										
5										
6										
7										
8										
9										
10										

Week 2	Practice Page 5B

$1 \times 9 =$ _____ $4 \times 1 =$ _____ $10 \times 3 =$ _____

$2 \times 7 =$ _____ $9 \times 3 =$ _____ $2 \times 3 =$ _____

$5 \times 3 =$ _____ $3 \times 2 =$ _____ $9 \times 2 =$ _____

$10 \times 1 =$ _____ $6 \times 3 =$ _____ $6 \times 1 =$ _____

$2 \times 5 =$ _____ $2 \times 10 =$ _____ $4 \times 3 =$ _____

$1 \times 3 =$ _____ $2 \times 2 =$ _____ $3 \times 8 =$ _____

$4 \times 2 =$ _____ $8 \times 1 =$ _____ $3 \times 1 =$ _____

$5 \times 1 =$ _____ $3 \times 3 =$ _____ $6 \times 2 =$ _____

$3 \times 7 =$ _____ $2 \times 8 =$ _____ $1 \times 7 =$ _____

Week 3	Practice Page 1A

$1 \times 2 =$ _____ $1 \times 4 =$ _____

$2 \times 2 =$ _____ $2 \times 4 =$ _____

$3 \times 2 =$ _____ $3 \times 4 =$ _____

$4 \times 2 =$ _____ $4 \times 4 =$ _____

$5 \times 2 =$ _____ $5 \times 4 =$ _____

$6 \times 2 =$ _____ $6 \times 4 =$ _____

$7 \times 2 =$ _____ $7 \times 4 =$ _____

$8 \times 2 =$ _____ $8 \times 4 =$ _____

$9 \times 2 =$ _____ $9 \times 4 =$ _____

$10 \times 2 =$ _____ $10 \times 4 =$ _____

Week 3	Practice Page 1B

$2 \times 1 =$ _____

$4 \times 1 =$ _____

$2 \times 2 =$ _____

$4 \times 2 =$ _____

$2 \times 3 =$ _____

$4 \times 3 =$ _____

$2 \times 4 =$ _____

$4 \times 4 =$ _____

$2 \times 5 =$ _____

$4 \times 5 =$ _____

$2 \times 6 =$ _____

$4 \times 6 =$ _____

$2 \times 7 =$ _____

$4 \times 7 =$ _____

$2 \times 8 =$ _____

$4 \times 8 =$ _____

$2 \times 9 =$ _____

$4 \times 9 =$ _____

$2 \times 10 =$ _____

$4 \times 10 =$ _____

Week 3	Practice Page 2A

$1 \times 4 =$ _____ $1 \times 3 =$ _____

$2 \times 4 =$ _____ $2 \times 3 =$ _____

$3 \times 4 =$ _____ $3 \times 3 =$ _____

$4 \times 4 =$ _____ $4 \times 3 =$ _____

$5 \times 4 =$ _____ $5 \times 3 =$ _____

$6 \times 4 =$ _____ $6 \times 3 =$ _____

$7 \times 4 =$ _____ $7 \times 3 =$ _____

$8 \times 4 =$ _____ $8 \times 3 =$ _____

$9 \times 4 =$ _____ $9 \times 3 =$ _____

$10 \times 4 =$ _____ $10 \times 3 =$ _____

Week 3	Practice Page 2B

$3 \times 4 =$ _____ $9 \times 4 =$ _____ $1 \times 4 =$ _____

$6 \times 4 =$ _____ $10 \times 4 =$ _____ $7 \times 4 =$ _____

$4 \times 4 =$ _____ $2 \times 4 =$ _____ $8 \times 4 =$ _____

$5 \times 4 =$ _____ $6 \times 3 =$ _____ $3 \times 9 =$ _____

$3 \times 3 =$ _____ $2 \times 3 =$ _____ $10 \times 3 =$ _____

$8 \times 4 =$ _____ $1 \times 4 =$ _____ $9 \times 4 =$ _____

$5 \times 2 =$ _____ $8 \times 1 =$ _____ $4 \times 4 =$ _____

$2 \times 4 =$ _____ $10 \times 4 =$ _____ $6 \times 4 =$ _____

$4 \times 3 =$ _____ $6 \times 1 =$ _____ $8 \times 3 =$ _____

| Week 3 | Practice Page 3A |

$1 \times 4 = $ _____ $1 \times 2 = $ _____

$2 \times 4 = $ _____ $2 \times 2 = $ _____

$3 \times 4 = $ _____ $3 \times 2 = $ _____

$4 \times 4 = $ _____ $4 \times 2 = $ _____

$5 \times 4 = $ _____ $5 \times 2 = $ _____

$6 \times 4 = $ _____ $6 \times 2 = $ _____

$7 \times 4 = $ _____ $7 \times 2 = $ _____

$8 \times 4 = $ _____ $8 \times 2 = $ _____

$9 \times 4 = $ _____ $9 \times 2 = $ _____

$10 \times 4 = $ _____ $10 \times 2 = $ _____

| Week 3 | | | Practice Page 3B | |

$$\begin{array}{r} 5 \\ \times\ 4 \\ \hline \end{array} \qquad \begin{array}{r} 10 \\ \times\ 4 \\ \hline \end{array} \qquad \begin{array}{r} 8 \\ \times\ 4 \\ \hline \end{array} \qquad \begin{array}{r} 7 \\ \times\ 4 \\ \hline \end{array} \qquad \begin{array}{r} 1 \\ \times\ 4 \\ \hline \end{array}$$

$$\begin{array}{r} 4 \\ \times\ 4 \\ \hline \end{array} \qquad \begin{array}{r} 6 \\ \times\ 4 \\ \hline \end{array} \qquad \begin{array}{r} 3 \\ \times\ 4 \\ \hline \end{array} \qquad \begin{array}{r} 2 \\ \times\ 4 \\ \hline \end{array} \qquad \begin{array}{r} 9 \\ \times\ 4 \\ \hline \end{array}$$

$$\begin{array}{r} 5 \\ \times\ 3 \\ \hline \end{array} \qquad \begin{array}{r} 7 \\ \times\ 3 \\ \hline \end{array} \qquad \begin{array}{r} 2 \\ \times\ 2 \\ \hline \end{array} \qquad \begin{array}{r} 3 \\ \times\ 4 \\ \hline \end{array} \qquad \begin{array}{r} 4 \\ \times\ 2 \\ \hline \end{array}$$

$$\begin{array}{r} 1 \\ \times\ 2 \\ \hline \end{array} \qquad \begin{array}{r} 4 \\ \times\ 7 \\ \hline \end{array} \qquad \begin{array}{r} 2 \\ \times\ 9 \\ \hline \end{array} \qquad \begin{array}{r} 1 \\ \times\ 3 \\ \hline \end{array} \qquad \begin{array}{r} 2 \\ \times\ 6 \\ \hline \end{array}$$

$$\begin{array}{r} 7 \\ \times\ 1 \\ \hline \end{array} \qquad \begin{array}{r} 10 \\ \times\ 1 \\ \hline \end{array} \qquad \begin{array}{r} 5 \\ \times\ 4 \\ \hline \end{array} \qquad \begin{array}{r} 7 \\ \times\ 2 \\ \hline \end{array} \qquad \begin{array}{r} 9 \\ \times\ 1 \\ \hline \end{array}$$

Week 3	Practice Page 4A

$1 \times 4 =$ _____ $1 \times 3 =$ _____

$2 \times 4 =$ _____ $2 \times 3 =$ _____

$3 \times 4 =$ _____ $3 \times 3 =$ _____

$4 \times 4 =$ _____ $4 \times 3 =$ _____

$5 \times 4 =$ _____ $5 \times 3 =$ _____

$6 \times 4 =$ _____ $6 \times 3 =$ _____

$7 \times 4 =$ _____ $7 \times 3 =$ _____

$8 \times 4 =$ _____ $8 \times 3 =$ _____

$9 \times 4 =$ _____ $9 \times 3 =$ _____

$10 \times 4 =$ _____ $10 \times 3 =$ _____

Week 3	Practice Page 4B

$5 \times 4 =$ _____ $4 \times 8 =$ _____ $2 \times 4 =$ _____

$4 \times 6 =$ _____ $4 \times 4 =$ _____ $3 \times 4 =$ _____

$4 \times 10 =$ _____ $1 \times 4 =$ _____ $7 \times 4 =$ _____

$9 \times 4 =$ _____ $3 \times 1 =$ _____ $2 \times 6 =$ _____

$10 \times 2 =$ _____ $8 \times 3 =$ _____ $6 \times 1 =$ _____

$3 \times 2 =$ _____ $3 \times 5 =$ _____ $1 \times 7 =$ _____

$2 \times 1 =$ _____ $4 \times 2 =$ _____ $5 \times 4 =$ _____

$8 \times 2 =$ _____ $7 \times 3 =$ _____ $10 \times 3 =$ _____

$1 \times 5 =$ _____ $4 \times 7 =$ _____ $2 \times 7 =$ _____

| Week 3 | Practice Page 5A |

×	1	2	3	4	5	6	7	8	9	10
1										
2										
3										
4										
5										
6										
7										
8										
9										
10										

Week 3	Practice Page 5B

$$
\begin{array}{r} 9 \\ \times\ 4 \\ \hline \end{array}
\qquad
\begin{array}{r} 3 \\ \times\ 9 \\ \hline \end{array}
\qquad
\begin{array}{r} 8 \\ \times\ 2 \\ \hline \end{array}
\qquad
\begin{array}{r} 6 \\ \times\ 4 \\ \hline \end{array}
\qquad
\begin{array}{r} 7 \\ \times\ 3 \\ \hline \end{array}
$$

$$
\begin{array}{r} 4 \\ \times\ 4 \\ \hline \end{array}
\qquad
\begin{array}{r} 3 \\ \times\ 3 \\ \hline \end{array}
\qquad
\begin{array}{r} 3 \\ \times\ 4 \\ \hline \end{array}
\qquad
\begin{array}{r} 4 \\ \times\ 2 \\ \hline \end{array}
\qquad
\begin{array}{r} 7 \\ \times\ 4 \\ \hline \end{array}
$$

$$
\begin{array}{r} 2 \\ \times\ 2 \\ \hline \end{array}
\qquad
\begin{array}{r} 8 \\ \times\ 4 \\ \hline \end{array}
\qquad
\begin{array}{r} 4 \\ \times\ 1 \\ \hline \end{array}
\qquad
\begin{array}{r} 2 \\ \times\ 3 \\ \hline \end{array}
\qquad
\begin{array}{r} 5 \\ \times\ 4 \\ \hline \end{array}
$$

$$
\begin{array}{r} 2 \\ \times\ 9 \\ \hline \end{array}
\qquad
\begin{array}{r} 10 \\ \times\ 2 \\ \hline \end{array}
\qquad
\begin{array}{r} 10 \\ \times\ 4 \\ \hline \end{array}
\qquad
\begin{array}{r} 8 \\ \times\ 3 \\ \hline \end{array}
\qquad
\begin{array}{r} 2 \\ \times\ 6 \\ \hline \end{array}
$$

$$
\begin{array}{r} 6 \\ \times\ 3 \\ \hline \end{array}
\qquad
\begin{array}{r} 3 \\ \times\ 2 \\ \hline \end{array}
\qquad
\begin{array}{r} 5 \\ \times\ 2 \\ \hline \end{array}
\qquad
\begin{array}{r} 5 \\ \times\ 3 \\ \hline \end{array}
\qquad
\begin{array}{r} 2 \\ \times\ 7 \\ \hline \end{array}
$$

Week 4	Practice Page 1A

$1 \times 10 = \underline{\hspace{2cm}}$ $1 \times 4 = \underline{\hspace{2cm}}$

$2 \times 10 = \underline{\hspace{2cm}}$ $2 \times 4 = \underline{\hspace{2cm}}$

$3 \times 10 = \underline{\hspace{2cm}}$ $3 \times 4 = \underline{\hspace{2cm}}$

$4 \times 10 = \underline{\hspace{2cm}}$ $4 \times 4 = \underline{\hspace{2cm}}$

$5 \times 10 = \underline{\hspace{2cm}}$ $5 \times 4 = \underline{\hspace{2cm}}$

$6 \times 10 = \underline{\hspace{2cm}}$ $6 \times 4 = \underline{\hspace{2cm}}$

$7 \times 10 = \underline{\hspace{2cm}}$ $7 \times 4 = \underline{\hspace{2cm}}$

$8 \times 10 = \underline{\hspace{2cm}}$ $8 \times 4 = \underline{\hspace{2cm}}$

$9 \times 10 = \underline{\hspace{2cm}}$ $9 \times 4 = \underline{\hspace{2cm}}$

$10 \times 10 = \underline{\hspace{2cm}}$ $10 \times 4 = \underline{\hspace{2cm}}$

Week 4	Practice Page 1B

$4 \times 10 =$ _____ $8 \times 10 =$ _____ $10 \times 10 =$ _____

$1 \times 10 =$ _____ $5 \times 10 =$ _____ $9 \times 10 =$ _____

$6 \times 10 =$ _____ $3 \times 10 =$ _____ $2 \times 10 =$ _____

$7 \times 10 =$ _____ $9 \times 2 =$ _____ $2 \times 5 =$ _____

$8 \times 2 =$ _____ $3 \times 9 =$ _____ $6 \times 3 =$ _____

$3 \times 5 =$ _____ $9 \times 4 =$ _____ $7 \times 3 =$ _____

$4 \times 6 =$ _____ $2 \times 6 =$ _____ $8 \times 4 =$ _____

$10 \times 2 =$ _____ $7 \times 2 =$ _____ $4 \times 5 =$ _____

$7 \times 4 =$ _____ $10 \times 3 =$ _____ $4 \times 10 =$ _____

Week 4	Practice Page 2A

$1 \times 10 =$ _____ $1 \times 3 =$ _____

$2 \times 10 =$ _____ $2 \times 3 =$ _____

$3 \times 10 =$ _____ $3 \times 3 =$ _____

$4 \times 10 =$ _____ $4 \times 3 =$ _____

$5 \times 10 =$ _____ $5 \times 3 =$ _____

$6 \times 10 =$ _____ $6 \times 3 =$ _____

$7 \times 10 =$ _____ $7 \times 3 =$ _____

$8 \times 10 =$ _____ $8 \times 3 =$ _____

$9 \times 10 =$ _____ $9 \times 3 =$ _____

$10 \times 10 =$ _____ $10 \times 3 =$ _____

Week 4	Practice Page 2B

$8 \times 10 =$ _____ $3 \times 10 =$ _____ $2 \times 10 =$ _____

$7 \times 10 =$ _____ $1 \times 10 =$ _____ $4 \times 10 =$ _____

$10 \times 10 =$ _____ $9 \times 10 =$ _____ $6 \times 10 =$ _____

$5 \times 10 =$ _____ $5 \times 3 =$ _____ $4 \times 3 =$ _____

$9 \times 2 =$ _____ $2 \times 6 =$ _____ $4 \times 4 =$ _____

$6 \times 4 =$ _____ $8 \times 4 =$ _____ $4 \times 2 =$ _____

$5 \times 4 =$ _____ $7 \times 3 =$ _____ $9 \times 4 =$ _____

$3 \times 9 =$ _____ $3 \times 4 =$ _____ $6 \times 3 =$ _____

$5 \times 2 =$ _____ $4 \times 2 =$ _____ $8 \times 3 =$ _____

| Week 4 | Practice Page 3A |

$1 \times 10 =$ _____ $1 \times 2 =$ _____

$2 \times 10 =$ _____ $2 \times 2 =$ _____

$3 \times 10 =$ _____ $3 \times 2 =$ _____

$4 \times 10 =$ _____ $4 \times 2 =$ _____

$5 \times 10 =$ _____ $5 \times 2 =$ _____

$6 \times 10 =$ _____ $6 \times 2 =$ _____

$7 \times 10 =$ _____ $7 \times 2 =$ _____

$8 \times 10 =$ _____ $8 \times 2 =$ _____

$9 \times 10 =$ _____ $9 \times 2 =$ _____

$10 \times 10 =$ _____ $10 \times 2 =$ _____

| Week 4 | Practice Page 3B |

$$\begin{array}{r} 3 \\ \times\ 10 \\ \hline \end{array}$$ $$\begin{array}{r} 10 \\ \times\ 10 \\ \hline \end{array}$$ $$\begin{array}{r} 1 \\ \times\ 10 \\ \hline \end{array}$$ $$\begin{array}{r} 4 \\ \times\ 10 \\ \hline \end{array}$$ $$\begin{array}{r} 5 \\ \times\ 10 \\ \hline \end{array}$$

$$\begin{array}{r} 2 \\ \times\ 10 \\ \hline \end{array}$$ $$\begin{array}{r} 6 \\ \times\ 10 \\ \hline \end{array}$$ $$\begin{array}{r} 8 \\ \times\ 10 \\ \hline \end{array}$$ $$\begin{array}{r} 9 \\ \times\ 10 \\ \hline \end{array}$$ $$\begin{array}{r} 2 \\ \times\ 10 \\ \hline \end{array}$$

$$\begin{array}{r} 7 \\ \times\ 3 \\ \hline \end{array}$$ $$\begin{array}{r} 2 \\ \times\ 4 \\ \hline \end{array}$$ $$\begin{array}{r} 3 \\ \times\ 6 \\ \hline \end{array}$$ $$\begin{array}{r} 6 \\ \times\ 4 \\ \hline \end{array}$$ $$\begin{array}{r} 3 \\ \times\ 9 \\ \hline \end{array}$$

$$\begin{array}{r} 4 \\ \times\ 5 \\ \hline \end{array}$$ $$\begin{array}{r} 8 \\ \times\ 3 \\ \hline \end{array}$$ $$\begin{array}{r} 4 \\ \times\ 4 \\ \hline \end{array}$$ $$\begin{array}{r} 10 \\ \times\ 3 \\ \hline \end{array}$$ $$\begin{array}{r} 4 \\ \times\ 3 \\ \hline \end{array}$$

$$\begin{array}{r} 8 \\ \times\ 2 \\ \hline \end{array}$$ $$\begin{array}{r} 7 \\ \times\ 4 \\ \hline \end{array}$$ $$\begin{array}{r} 8 \\ \times\ 4 \\ \hline \end{array}$$ $$\begin{array}{r} 2 \\ \times\ 7 \\ \hline \end{array}$$ $$\begin{array}{r} 5 \\ \times\ 3 \\ \hline \end{array}$$

Week 4	Practice Page 4A

1 × 10 = _____   1 × 4 = _____

2 × 10 = _____   2 × 4 = _____

3 × 10 = _____   3 × 4 = _____

4 × 10 = _____   4 × 4 = _____

5 × 10 = _____   5 × 4 = _____

6 × 10 = _____   6 × 4 = _____

7 × 10 = _____   7 × 4 = _____

8 × 10 = _____   8 × 4 = _____

9 × 10 = _____   9 × 4 = _____

10 × 10 = _____   10 × 4 = _____

Week 4	Practice Page 4B

$1 \times 10 =$ _____ $10 \times 9 =$ _____ $6 \times 10 =$ _____

$2 \times 10 =$ _____ $10 \times 10 =$ _____ $10 \times 8 =$ _____

$10 \times 4 =$ _____ $5 \times 10 =$ _____ $7 \times 10 =$ _____

$10 \times 3 =$ _____ $9 \times 4 =$ _____ $2 \times 2 =$ _____

$8 \times 3 =$ _____ $3 \times 3 =$ _____ $6 \times 3 =$ _____

$9 \times 3 =$ _____ $8 \times 4 =$ _____ $6 \times 4 =$ _____

$8 \times 4 =$ _____ $4 \times 2 =$ _____ $9 \times 4 =$ _____

$7 \times 3 =$ _____ $4 \times 3 =$ _____ $2 \times 8 =$ _____

$4 \times 7 =$ _____ $7 \times 4 =$ _____ $3 \times 2 =$ _____

Week 4   **Practice Page 5A**

×	1	2	3	4	5	6	7	8	9	10
1										
2										
3										
4										
5										
6										
7										
8										
9										
10										

Week 4	Practice Page 5B

$$\begin{array}{r} 7 \\ \times\ 10 \\ \hline \end{array} \qquad \begin{array}{r} 3 \\ \times\ 7 \\ \hline \end{array} \qquad \begin{array}{r} 5 \\ \times\ 4 \\ \hline \end{array} \qquad \begin{array}{r} 3 \\ \times\ 10 \\ \hline \end{array} \qquad \begin{array}{r} 10 \\ \times\ 2 \\ \hline \end{array}$$

$$\begin{array}{r} 8 \\ \times\ 4 \\ \hline \end{array} \qquad \begin{array}{r} 10 \\ \times\ 6 \\ \hline \end{array} \qquad \begin{array}{r} 3 \\ \times\ 5 \\ \hline \end{array} \qquad \begin{array}{r} 2 \\ \times\ 9 \\ \hline \end{array} \qquad \begin{array}{r} 6 \\ \times\ 3 \\ \hline \end{array}$$

$$\begin{array}{r} 1 \\ \times\ 10 \\ \hline \end{array} \qquad \begin{array}{r} 7 \\ \times\ 4 \\ \hline \end{array} \qquad \begin{array}{r} 4 \\ \times\ 4 \\ \hline \end{array} \qquad \begin{array}{r} 9 \\ \times\ 3 \\ \hline \end{array} \qquad \begin{array}{r} 4 \\ \times\ 10 \\ \hline \end{array}$$

$$\begin{array}{r} 4 \\ \times\ 6 \\ \hline \end{array} \qquad \begin{array}{r} 10 \\ \times\ 3 \\ \hline \end{array} \qquad \begin{array}{r} 8 \\ \times\ 2 \\ \hline \end{array} \qquad \begin{array}{r} 10 \\ \times\ 10 \\ \hline \end{array} \qquad \begin{array}{r} 9 \\ \times\ 4 \\ \hline \end{array}$$

$$\begin{array}{r} 9 \\ \times\ 10 \\ \hline \end{array} \qquad \begin{array}{r} 5 \\ \times\ 10 \\ \hline \end{array} \qquad \begin{array}{r} 4 \\ \times\ 5 \\ \hline \end{array} \qquad \begin{array}{r} 8 \\ \times\ 3 \\ \hline \end{array} \qquad \begin{array}{r} 8 \\ \times\ 10 \\ \hline \end{array}$$

| Week 5 | Practice Page 1A |

$1 \times 5 =$ _____ $1 \times 10 =$ _____

$2 \times 5 =$ _____ $2 \times 10 =$ _____

$3 \times 5 =$ _____ $3 \times 10 =$ _____

$4 \times 5 =$ _____ $4 \times 10 =$ _____

$5 \times 5 =$ _____ $5 \times 10 =$ _____

$6 \times 5 =$ _____ $6 \times 10 =$ _____

$7 \times 5 =$ _____ $7 \times 10 =$ _____

$8 \times 5 =$ _____ $8 \times 10 =$ _____

$9 \times 5 =$ _____ $9 \times 10 =$ _____

$10 \times 5 =$ _____ $10 \times 10 =$ _____

Week 5	Practice Page 1B

$3 \times 5 =$ _____ $9 \times 5 =$ _____ $1 \times 5 =$ _____

$6 \times 5 =$ _____ $10 \times 5 =$ _____ $7 \times 5 =$ _____

$4 \times 5 =$ _____ $2 \times 5 =$ _____ $8 \times 5 =$ _____

$5 \times 5 =$ _____ $3 \times 8 =$ _____ $7 \times 2 =$ _____

$9 \times 3 =$ _____ $2 \times 10 =$ _____ $9 \times 4 =$ _____

$7 \times 4 =$ _____ $5 \times 4 =$ _____ $2 \times 9 =$ _____

$3 \times 7 =$ _____ $4 \times 4 =$ _____ $10 \times 10 =$ _____

$5 \times 3 =$ _____ $10 \times 3 =$ _____ $8 \times 2 =$ _____

$6 \times 10 =$ _____ $6 \times 3 =$ _____ $4 \times 10 =$ _____

| Week 5 | Practice Page 2A |

$1 \times 5 =$ _____ $1 \times 3 =$ _____

$2 \times 5 =$ _____ $2 \times 3 =$ _____

$3 \times 5 =$ _____ $3 \times 3 =$ _____

$4 \times 5 =$ _____ $4 \times 3 =$ _____

$5 \times 5 =$ _____ $5 \times 3 =$ _____

$6 \times 5 =$ _____ $6 \times 3 =$ _____

$7 \times 5 =$ _____ $7 \times 3 =$ _____

$8 \times 5 =$ _____ $8 \times 3 =$ _____

$9 \times 5 =$ _____ $9 \times 3 =$ _____

$10 \times 5 =$ _____ $10 \times 3 =$ _____

Week 5	Practice Page 2B

$5 \times 5 =$ _____ $3 \times 5 =$ _____ $2 \times 5 =$ _____

$8 \times 5 =$ _____ $1 \times 5 =$ _____ $4 \times 5 =$ _____

$10 \times 5 =$ _____ $9 \times 5 =$ _____ $6 \times 5 =$ _____

$7 \times 5 =$ _____ $6 \times 2 =$ _____ $10 \times 2 =$ _____

$9 \times 10 =$ _____ $7 \times 3 =$ _____ $8 \times 3 =$ _____

$8 \times 4 =$ _____ $2 \times 8 =$ _____ $3 \times 4 =$ _____

$3 \times 3 =$ _____ $7 \times 2 =$ _____ $10 \times 3 =$ _____

$6 \times 4 =$ _____ $5 \times 4 =$ _____ $7 \times 10 =$ _____

$9 \times 3 =$ _____ $8 \times 10 =$ _____ $2 \times 9 =$ _____

Week 5	Practice Page 3A

$1 \times 5 =$ _____ $1 \times 10 =$ _____

$2 \times 5 =$ _____ $2 \times 10 =$ _____

$3 \times 5 =$ _____ $3 \times 10 =$ _____

$4 \times 5 =$ _____ $4 \times 10 =$ _____

$5 \times 5 =$ _____ $5 \times 10 =$ _____

$6 \times 5 =$ _____ $6 \times 10 =$ _____

$7 \times 5 =$ _____ $7 \times 10 =$ _____

$8 \times 5 =$ _____ $8 \times 10 =$ _____

$9 \times 5 =$ _____ $9 \times 10 =$ _____

$10 \times 5 =$ _____ $10 \times 10 =$ _____

| Week 5 | Practice Page 3B |

$$
\begin{array}{r} 1 \\ \times\ 5 \\ \hline \end{array}
\qquad
\begin{array}{r} 10 \\ \times\ 5 \\ \hline \end{array}
\qquad
\begin{array}{r} 3 \\ \times\ 5 \\ \hline \end{array}
\qquad
\begin{array}{r} 5 \\ \times\ 5 \\ \hline \end{array}
\qquad
\begin{array}{r} 4 \\ \times\ 5 \\ \hline \end{array}
$$

$$
\begin{array}{r} 7 \\ \times\ 5 \\ \hline \end{array}
\qquad
\begin{array}{r} 6 \\ \times\ 5 \\ \hline \end{array}
\qquad
\begin{array}{r} 8 \\ \times\ 5 \\ \hline \end{array}
\qquad
\begin{array}{r} 9 \\ \times\ 5 \\ \hline \end{array}
\qquad
\begin{array}{r} 2 \\ \times\ 5 \\ \hline \end{array}
$$

$$
\begin{array}{r} 8 \\ \times\ 4 \\ \hline \end{array}
\qquad
\begin{array}{r} 10 \\ \times\ 4 \\ \hline \end{array}
\qquad
\begin{array}{r} 4 \\ \times\ 3 \\ \hline \end{array}
\qquad
\begin{array}{r} 3 \\ \times\ 8 \\ \hline \end{array}
\qquad
\begin{array}{r} 7 \\ \times\ 2 \\ \hline \end{array}
$$

$$
\begin{array}{r} 5 \\ \times\ 3 \\ \hline \end{array}
\qquad
\begin{array}{r} 4 \\ \times\ 7 \\ \hline \end{array}
\qquad
\begin{array}{r} 2 \\ \times\ 4 \\ \hline \end{array}
\qquad
\begin{array}{r} 10 \\ \times\ 7 \\ \hline \end{array}
\qquad
\begin{array}{r} 2 \\ \times\ 8 \\ \hline \end{array}
$$

$$
\begin{array}{r} 9 \\ \times\ 4 \\ \hline \end{array}
\qquad
\begin{array}{r} 10 \\ \times\ 10 \\ \hline \end{array}
\qquad
\begin{array}{r} 5 \\ \times\ 4 \\ \hline \end{array}
\qquad
\begin{array}{r} 2 \\ \times\ 6 \\ \hline \end{array}
\qquad
\begin{array}{r} 9 \\ \times\ 5 \\ \hline \end{array}
$$

Week 5	Practice Page 4A

$1 \times 5 =$ _____ $1 \times 4 =$ _____

$2 \times 5 =$ _____ $2 \times 4 =$ _____

$3 \times 5 =$ _____ $3 \times 4 =$ _____

$4 \times 5 =$ _____ $4 \times 4 =$ _____

$5 \times 5 =$ _____ $5 \times 4 =$ _____

$6 \times 5 =$ _____ $6 \times 4 =$ _____

$7 \times 5 =$ _____ $7 \times 4 =$ _____

$8 \times 5 =$ _____ $8 \times 4 =$ _____

$9 \times 5 =$ _____ $9 \times 4 =$ _____

$10 \times 5 =$ _____ $10 \times 4 =$ _____

Week 5		Practice Page 4B

$1 \times 5 =$ _____ $5 \times 9 =$ _____ $6 \times 5 =$ _____

$2 \times 5 =$ _____ $10 \times 5 =$ _____ $5 \times 8 =$ _____

$5 \times 4 =$ _____ $5 \times 5 =$ _____ $7 \times 5 =$ _____

$3 \times 5 =$ _____ $9 \times 2 =$ _____ $3 \times 9 =$ _____

$6 \times 4 =$ _____ $5 \times 10 =$ _____ $3 \times 4 =$ _____

$5 \times 7 =$ _____ $4 \times 5 =$ _____ $3 \times 7 =$ _____

$10 \times 9 =$ _____ $5 \times 5 =$ _____ $8 \times 10 =$ _____

$3 \times 5 =$ _____ $8 \times 4 =$ _____ $3 \times 3 =$ _____

$4 \times 10 =$ _____ $4 \times 7 =$ _____ $4 \times 4 =$ _____

Week 5	Practice Page 5A

×	1	2	3	4	5	6	7	8	9	10
1										
2										
3										
4										
5										
6										
7										
8										
9										
10										

Week 5		Practice Page 5B

$$\begin{array}{r} 8 \\ \times\ 5 \\ \hline \end{array} \qquad \begin{array}{r} 4 \\ \times\ 5 \\ \hline \end{array} \qquad \begin{array}{r} 8 \\ \times\ 2 \\ \hline \end{array} \qquad \begin{array}{r} 6 \\ \times\ 4 \\ \hline \end{array} \qquad \begin{array}{r} 10 \\ \times\ 6 \\ \hline \end{array}$$

$$\begin{array}{r} 9 \\ \times\ 4 \\ \hline \end{array} \qquad \begin{array}{r} 3 \\ \times\ 6 \\ \hline \end{array} \qquad \begin{array}{r} 10 \\ \times\ 4 \\ \hline \end{array} \qquad \begin{array}{r} 8 \\ \times\ 3 \\ \hline \end{array} \qquad \begin{array}{r} 5 \\ \times\ 1 \\ \hline \end{array}$$

$$\begin{array}{r} 5 \\ \times\ 6 \\ \hline \end{array} \qquad \begin{array}{r} 5 \\ \times\ 5 \\ \hline \end{array} \qquad \begin{array}{r} 10 \\ \times\ 5 \\ \hline \end{array} \qquad \begin{array}{r} 7 \\ \times\ 4 \\ \hline \end{array} \qquad \begin{array}{r} 5 \\ \times\ 4 \\ \hline \end{array}$$

$$\begin{array}{r} 4 \\ \times\ 4 \\ \hline \end{array} \qquad \begin{array}{r} 10 \\ \times\ 3 \\ \hline \end{array} \qquad \begin{array}{r} 7 \\ \times\ 5 \\ \hline \end{array} \qquad \begin{array}{r} 5 \\ \times\ 9 \\ \hline \end{array} \qquad \begin{array}{r} 4 \\ \times\ 3 \\ \hline \end{array}$$

$$\begin{array}{r} 3 \\ \times\ 5 \\ \hline \end{array} \qquad \begin{array}{r} 7 \\ \times\ 3 \\ \hline \end{array} \qquad \begin{array}{r} 4 \\ \times\ 8 \\ \hline \end{array} \qquad \begin{array}{r} 7 \\ \times\ 2 \\ \hline \end{array} \qquad \begin{array}{r} 9 \\ \times\ 3 \\ \hline \end{array}$$

| Week 6 | Practice Page 1A |

1 × 6 = _____   1 × 5 = _____

2 × 6= _____   2 × 5 = _____

3 × 6 = _____   3 × 5 = _____

4 × 6 = _____   4 × 5 = _____

5 × 6 = _____   5 × 5 = _____

6 × 6 = _____   6 × 5 = _____

7 × 6 = _____   7 × 5 = _____

8 × 6 = _____   8 × 5 = _____

9 × 6 = _____   9 × 5 = _____

10 × 6 = _____   10 × 5 = _____

Week 6	Practice Page 1B

$5 \times 1 =$ _____ $6 \times 1 =$ _____	$5 \times 2 =$ _____ $6 \times 2 =$ _____	$5 \times 3 =$ _____ $6 \times 3 =$ _____
$5 \times 4 =$ _____ $6 \times 4 =$ _____	$5 \times 5 =$ _____ $6 \times 5 =$ _____	$5 \times 6 =$ _____ $6 \times 6 =$ _____
$5 \times 7 =$ _____ $6 \times 7 =$ _____	$5 \times 8 =$ _____ $6 \times 8 =$ _____	$5 \times 9 =$ _____ $6 \times 9 =$ _____
$5 \times 10 =$ _____ $6 \times 10 =$ _____		

Week 6	Practice Page 2A

$1 \times 6 =$ _____ $1 \times 10 =$ _____

$2 \times 6 =$ _____ $2 \times 10 =$ _____

$3 \times 6 =$ _____ $3 \times 10 =$ _____

$4 \times 6 =$ _____ $4 \times 10 =$ _____

$5 \times 6 =$ _____ $5 \times 10 =$ _____

$6 \times 6 =$ _____ $6 \times 10 =$ _____

$7 \times 6 =$ _____ $7 \times 10 =$ _____

$8 \times 6 =$ _____ $8 \times 10 =$ _____

$9 \times 6 =$ _____ $9 \times 10 =$ _____

$10 \times 6 =$ _____ $10 \times 10 =$ _____

Week 6	Practice Page 2B

$5 \times 6 =$ _____ $3 \times 6 =$ _____ $2 \times 6 =$ _____

$8 \times 6 =$ _____ $1 \times 6 =$ _____ $4 \times 6 =$ _____

$10 \times 6 =$ _____ $9 \times 6 =$ _____ $6 \times 6 =$ _____

$7 \times 6 =$ _____ $9 \times 4 =$ _____ $7 \times 3 =$ _____

$5 \times 7 =$ _____ $7 \times 4 =$ _____ $9 \times 5 =$ _____

$3 \times 9 =$ _____ $8 \times 4 =$ _____ $8 \times 5 =$ _____

$5 \times 5 =$ _____ $9 \times 2 =$ _____ $10 \times 3 =$ _____

$2 \times 8 =$ _____ $5 \times 10 =$ _____ $10 \times 9 =$ _____

$5 \times 4 =$ _____ $10 \times 8 =$ _____ $8 \times 3 =$ _____

Week 6	Practice Page 3A

$1 \times 6 =$ _____ $1 \times 3 =$ _____

$2 \times 6 =$ _____ $2 \times 3 =$ _____

$3 \times 6 =$ _____ $3 \times 3 =$ _____

$4 \times 6 =$ _____ $4 \times 3 =$ _____

$5 \times 6 =$ _____ $5 \times 3 =$ _____

$6 \times 6 =$ _____ $6 \times 3 =$ _____

$7 \times 6 =$ _____ $7 \times 3 =$ _____

$8 \times 6 =$ _____ $8 \times 3 =$ _____

$9 \times 6 =$ _____ $9 \times 3 =$ _____

$10 \times 6 =$ _____ $10 \times 3 =$ _____

Week 6	Practice Page 3B

$$
\begin{array}{ccccc}
1 & 10 & 3 & 5 & 4 \\
\times\ 6 & \times\ 6 & \times\ 6 & \times\ 6 & \times\ 6 \\
\hline
\end{array}
$$

$$
\begin{array}{ccccc}
7 & 6 & 8 & 9 & 2 \\
\times\ 6 & \times\ 6 & \times\ 6 & \times\ 6 & \times\ 6 \\
\hline
\end{array}
$$

$$
\begin{array}{ccccc}
9 & 2 & 7 & 5 & 10 \\
\times\ 3 & \times\ 5 & \times\ 2 & \times\ 9 & \times\ 4 \\
\hline
\end{array}
$$

$$
\begin{array}{ccccc}
8 & 5 & 9 & 3 & 7 \\
\times\ 4 & \times\ 3 & \times\ 6 & \times\ 7 & \times\ 10 \\
\hline
\end{array}
$$

$$
\begin{array}{ccccc}
7 & 8 & 7 & 4 & 6 \\
\times\ 5 & \times\ 3 & \times\ 4 & \times\ 9 & \times\ 8 \\
\hline
\end{array}
$$

| Week 6 | Practice Page 4A |

$1 \times 6 =$ _____ $\qquad$ $1 \times 5 =$ _____

$2 \times 6 =$ _____ $\qquad$ $2 \times 5 =$ _____

$3 \times 6 =$ _____ $\qquad$ $3 \times 5 =$ _____

$4 \times 6 =$ _____ $\qquad$ $4 \times 5 =$ _____

$5 \times 6 =$ _____ $\qquad$ $5 \times 5 =$ _____

$6 \times 6 =$ _____ $\qquad$ $6 \times 5 =$ _____

$7 \times 6 =$ _____ $\qquad$ $7 \times 5 =$ _____

$8 \times 6 =$ _____ $\qquad$ $8 \times 5 =$ _____

$9 \times 6 =$ _____ $\qquad$ $9 \times 5 =$ _____

$10 \times 6 =$ _____ $\qquad$ $10 \times 5 =$ _____

| Week 6 | Practice Page 4B |

$1 \times 6 =$ _____ $6 \times 9 =$ _____ $6 \times 6 =$ _____

$2 \times 6 =$ _____ $10 \times 6 =$ _____ $6 \times 8 =$ _____

$6 \times 4 =$ _____ $5 \times 6 =$ _____ $7 \times 6 =$ _____

$3 \times 6 =$ _____ $10 \times 8 =$ _____ $2 \times 2 =$ _____

$10 \times 2 =$ _____ $9 \times 5 =$ _____ $10 \times 4 =$ _____

$5 \times 4 =$ _____ $4 \times 5 =$ _____ $2 \times 7 =$ _____

$8 \times 5 =$ _____ $10 \times 10 =$ _____ $6 \times 5 =$ _____

$2 \times 4 =$ _____ $8 \times 2 =$ _____ $3 \times 3 =$ _____

$5 \times 10 =$ _____ $6 \times 3 =$ _____ $4 \times 6 =$ _____

Week 6									Practice Page 5A

×	1	2	3	4	5	6	7	8	9	10
1										
2										
3										
4										
5										
6										
7										
8										
9										
10										

Week 6	Practice Page 5B

$$\begin{array}{r} 2 \\ \times\ 6 \\ \hline \end{array}$$ $$\begin{array}{r} 3 \\ \times\ 5 \\ \hline \end{array}$$ $$\begin{array}{r} 8 \\ \times\ 2 \\ \hline \end{array}$$ $$\begin{array}{r} 5 \\ \times\ 6 \\ \hline \end{array}$$ $$\begin{array}{r} 10 \\ \times\ 9 \\ \hline \end{array}$$

$$\begin{array}{r} 8 \\ \times\ 4 \\ \hline \end{array}$$ $$\begin{array}{r} 3 \\ \times\ 6 \\ \hline \end{array}$$ $$\begin{array}{r} 10 \\ \times\ 6 \\ \hline \end{array}$$ $$\begin{array}{r} 8 \\ \times\ 3 \\ \hline \end{array}$$ $$\begin{array}{r} 6 \\ \times\ 1 \\ \hline \end{array}$$

$$\begin{array}{r} 8 \\ \times\ 3 \\ \hline \end{array}$$ $$\begin{array}{r} 8 \\ \times\ 6 \\ \hline \end{array}$$ $$\begin{array}{r} 4 \\ \times\ 7 \\ \hline \end{array}$$ $$\begin{array}{r} 9 \\ \times\ 4 \\ \hline \end{array}$$ $$\begin{array}{r} 4 \\ \times\ 6 \\ \hline \end{array}$$

$$\begin{array}{r} 7 \\ \times\ 5 \\ \hline \end{array}$$ $$\begin{array}{r} 10 \\ \times\ 3 \\ \hline \end{array}$$ $$\begin{array}{r} 7 \\ \times\ 6 \\ \hline \end{array}$$ $$\begin{array}{r} 5 \\ \times\ 3 \\ \hline \end{array}$$ $$\begin{array}{r} 9 \\ \times\ 6 \\ \hline \end{array}$$

$$\begin{array}{r} 9 \\ \times\ 3 \\ \hline \end{array}$$ $$\begin{array}{r} 5 \\ \times\ 5 \\ \hline \end{array}$$ $$\begin{array}{r} 4 \\ \times\ 8 \\ \hline \end{array}$$ $$\begin{array}{r} 4 \\ \times\ 4 \\ \hline \end{array}$$ $$\begin{array}{r} 10 \\ \times\ 10 \\ \hline \end{array}$$

Week 7	Practice Page 1A

$1 \times 9 =$ _____ $1 \times 10 =$ _____

$2 \times 9 =$ _____ $2 \times 10 =$ _____

$3 \times 9 =$ _____ $3 \times 10 =$ _____

$4 \times 9 =$ _____ $4 \times 10 =$ _____

$5 \times 9 =$ _____ $5 \times 10 =$ _____

$6 \times 9 =$ _____ $6 \times 10 =$ _____

$7 \times 9 =$ _____ $7 \times 10 =$ _____

$8 \times 9 =$ _____ $8 \times 10 =$ _____

$9 \times 9 =$ _____ $9 \times 10 =$ _____

$10 \times 9 =$ _____ $10 \times 10 =$ _____

Week 7	Practice Page 1B

$10 \times 1 =$ _____ $9 \times 1 =$ _____	$10 \times 2 =$ _____ $9 \times 2 =$ _____	$10 \times 3 =$ _____ $9 \times 3 =$ _____
$10 \times 4 =$ _____ $9 \times 4 =$ _____	$10 \times 5 =$ _____ $9 \times 5 =$ _____	$10 \times 6 =$ _____ $9 \times 6 =$ _____
$10 \times 7 =$ _____ $9 \times 7 =$ _____	$10 \times 8 =$ _____ $9 \times 8 =$ _____	$10 \times 9 =$ _____ $9 \times 9 =$ _____
$10 \times 10 =$ _____ $9 \times 10 =$ _____		

| Week 7 | Practice Page 2A |

$1 \times 9 = \underline{\hspace{1cm}}$ $1 \times 6 = \underline{\hspace{1cm}}$

$2 \times 9 = \underline{\hspace{1cm}}$ $2 \times 6 = \underline{\hspace{1cm}}$

$3 \times 9 = \underline{\hspace{1cm}}$ $3 \times 6 = \underline{\hspace{1cm}}$

$4 \times 9 = \underline{\hspace{1cm}}$ $4 \times 6 = \underline{\hspace{1cm}}$

$5 \times 9 = \underline{\hspace{1cm}}$ $5 \times 6 = \underline{\hspace{1cm}}$

$6 \times 9 = \underline{\hspace{1cm}}$ $6 \times 6 = \underline{\hspace{1cm}}$

$7 \times 9 = \underline{\hspace{1cm}}$ $7 \times 6 = \underline{\hspace{1cm}}$

$8 \times 9 = \underline{\hspace{1cm}}$ $8 \times 6 = \underline{\hspace{1cm}}$

$9 \times 9 = \underline{\hspace{1cm}}$ $9 \times 6 = \underline{\hspace{1cm}}$

$10 \times 9 = \underline{\hspace{1cm}}$ $10 \times 6 = \underline{\hspace{1cm}}$

Week 7		Practice Page 2B

$2 \times 9 =$ _____ $3 \times 9 =$ _____ $8 \times 9 =$ _____

$7 \times 9 =$ _____ $10 \times 9 =$ _____ $6 \times 9 =$ _____

$1 \times 9 =$ _____ $8 \times 6 =$ _____ $8 \times 3 =$ _____

$7 \times 3 =$ _____ $4 \times 8 =$ _____ $7 \times 6 =$ _____

$8 \times 10 =$ _____ $6 \times 4 =$ _____ $7 \times 4 =$ _____

$6 \times 3 =$ _____ $7 \times 5 =$ _____ $4 \times 10 =$ _____

$5 \times 5 =$ _____ $10 \times 5 =$ _____ $4 \times 4 =$ _____

$3 \times 5 =$ _____ $8 \times 2 =$ _____ $2 \times 10 =$ _____

$5 \times 10 =$ _____ $5 \times 4 =$ _____ $6 \times 5 =$ _____

| Week 7 | Practice Page 3A |

$1 \times 9 =$ _____ $1 \times 4 =$ _____

$2 \times 9 =$ _____ $2 \times 4 =$ _____

$3 \times 9 =$ _____ $3 \times 4 =$ _____

$4 \times 9 =$ _____ $4 \times 4 =$ _____

$5 \times 9 =$ _____ $5 \times 4 =$ _____

$6 \times 9 =$ _____ $6 \times 4 =$ _____

$7 \times 9 =$ _____ $7 \times 4 =$ _____

$8 \times 9 =$ _____ $8 \times 4 =$ _____

$9 \times 9 =$ _____ $9 \times 4 =$ _____

$10 \times 9 =$ _____ $10 \times 4 =$ _____

| Week 7 | | | | Practice Page 3B |

$$
\begin{array}{ccccc}
3 & 10 & 1 & 4 & 5 \\
\times\,9 & \times\,9 & \times\,9 & \times\,9 & \times\,9 \\
\end{array}
$$

$$
\begin{array}{ccccc}
2 & 6 & 8 & 9 & 2 \\
\times\,9 & \times\,9 & \times\,9 & \times\,9 & \times\,9 \\
\end{array}
$$

$$
\begin{array}{ccccc}
6 & 6 & 4 & 7 & 3 \\
\times\,5 & \times\,10 & \times\,3 & \times\,5 & \times\,9 \\
\end{array}
$$

$$
\begin{array}{ccccc}
7 & 6 & 8 & 7 & 7 \\
\times\,4 & \times\,6 & \times\,4 & \times\,6 & \times\,3 \\
\end{array}
$$

$$
\begin{array}{ccccc}
8 & 7 & 4 & 5 & 6 \\
\times\,6 & \times\,10 & \times\,6 & \times\,8 & \times\,2 \\
\end{array}
$$

Week 7	Practice Page 4A

$1 \times 9 =$ _____ $1 \times 6 =$ _____

$2 \times 9 =$ _____ $2 \times 6 =$ _____

$3 \times 9 =$ _____ $3 \times 6 =$ _____

$4 \times 9 =$ _____ $4 \times 6 =$ _____

$5 \times 9 =$ _____ $5 \times 6 =$ _____

$6 \times 9 =$ _____ $6 \times 6 =$ _____

$7 \times 9 =$ _____ $7 \times 6 =$ _____

$8 \times 9 =$ _____ $8 \times 6 =$ _____

$9 \times 9 =$ _____ $9 \times 6 =$ _____

$10 \times 9 =$ _____ $10 \times 6 =$ _____

Week 7	Practice Page 4B

$1 \times 9 =$ _____ $9 \times 9 =$ _____ $6 \times 9 =$ _____

$2 \times 9 =$ _____ $10 \times 9 =$ _____ $9 \times 8 =$ _____

$9 \times 4 =$ _____ $5 \times 9 =$ _____ $7 \times 9 =$ _____

$9 \times 3 =$ _____ $3 \times 4 =$ _____ $5 \times 7 =$ _____

$8 \times 3 =$ _____ $10 \times 4 =$ _____ $4 \times 3 =$ _____

$5 \times 6 =$ _____ $7 \times 4 =$ _____ $3 \times 3 =$ _____

$10 \times 10 =$ _____ $8 \times 6 =$ _____ $6 \times 6 =$ _____

$8 \times 4 =$ _____ $7 \times 5 =$ _____ $2 \times 10 =$ _____

$5 \times 10 =$ _____ $6 \times 3 =$ _____ $4 \times 6 =$ _____

Week 7	Practice Page 5A

×	1	2	3	4	5	6	7	8	9	10
1										
2										
3										
4										
5										
6										
7										
8										
9										
10										

| Week 7 | | | | Practice Page 5B |

$$\begin{array}{r} 7 \\ \times\ 9 \\ \hline \end{array} \qquad \begin{array}{r} 3 \\ \times\ 8 \\ \hline \end{array} \qquad \begin{array}{r} 7 \\ \times\ 3 \\ \hline \end{array} \qquad \begin{array}{r} 6 \\ \times\ 7 \\ \hline \end{array} \qquad \begin{array}{r} 9 \\ \times\ 2 \\ \hline \end{array}$$

$$\begin{array}{r} 8 \\ \times\ 6 \\ \hline \end{array} \qquad \begin{array}{r} 9 \\ \times\ 6 \\ \hline \end{array} \qquad \begin{array}{r} 6 \\ \times\ 6 \\ \hline \end{array} \qquad \begin{array}{r} 7 \\ \times\ 4 \\ \hline \end{array} \qquad \begin{array}{r} 3 \\ \times\ 10 \\ \hline \end{array}$$

$$\begin{array}{r} 4 \\ \times\ 2 \\ \hline \end{array} \qquad \begin{array}{r} 7 \\ \times\ 5 \\ \hline \end{array} \qquad \begin{array}{r} 8 \\ \times\ 4 \\ \hline \end{array} \qquad \begin{array}{r} 2 \\ \times\ 5 \\ \hline \end{array} \qquad \begin{array}{r} 4 \\ \times\ 5 \\ \hline \end{array}$$

$$\begin{array}{r} 4 \\ \times\ 6 \\ \hline \end{array} \qquad \begin{array}{r} 9 \\ \times\ 3 \\ \hline \end{array} \qquad \begin{array}{r} 8 \\ \times\ 10 \\ \hline \end{array} \qquad \begin{array}{r} 10 \\ \times\ 9 \\ \hline \end{array} \qquad \begin{array}{r} 9 \\ \times\ 4 \\ \hline \end{array}$$

$$\begin{array}{r} 9 \\ \times\ 9 \\ \hline \end{array} \qquad \begin{array}{r} 5 \\ \times\ 9 \\ \hline \end{array} \qquad \begin{array}{r} 6 \\ \times\ 5 \\ \hline \end{array} \qquad \begin{array}{r} 5 \\ \times\ 3 \\ \hline \end{array} \qquad \begin{array}{r} 8 \\ \times\ 9 \\ \hline \end{array}$$

| Week 8 | Practice Page 1A |

$1 \times 7 =$ _____ $1 \times 5 =$ _____

$2 \times 7 =$ _____ $2 \times 5 =$ _____

$3 \times 7 =$ _____ $3 \times 5 =$ _____

$4 \times 7 =$ _____ $4 \times 5 =$ _____

$5 \times 7 =$ _____ $5 \times 5 =$ _____

$6 \times 7 =$ _____ $6 \times 5 =$ _____

$7 \times 7 =$ _____ $7 \times 5 =$ _____

$8 \times 7 =$ _____ $8 \times 5 =$ _____

$9 \times 7 =$ _____ $9 \times 5 =$ _____

$10 \times 7 =$ _____ $10 \times 5 =$ _____

Week 8	Practice Page 1B

$4 \times 7 =$ _____ $8 \times 7 =$ _____ $10 \times 7 =$ _____

$1 \times 7 =$ _____ $5 \times 7 =$ _____ $9 \times 7 =$ _____

$6 \times 7 =$ _____ $3 \times 7 =$ _____ $2 \times 7 =$ _____

$7 \times 7 =$ _____ $9 \times 6 =$ _____ $8 \times 4 =$ _____

$8 \times 9 =$ _____ $6 \times 6 =$ _____ $9 \times 3 =$ _____

$8 \times 6 =$ _____ $9 \times 4 =$ _____ $7 \times 3 =$ _____

$9 \times 5 =$ _____ $9 \times 9 =$ _____ $4 \times 9 =$ _____

$7 \times 5 =$ _____ $7 \times 9 =$ _____ $4 \times 10 =$ _____

$7 \times 2 =$ _____ $10 \times 10 =$ _____ $5 \times 6 =$ _____

| Week 8 | Practice Page 2A |

$1 \times 7 =$ _____

$2 \times 7 =$ _____

$3 \times 7 =$ _____

$4 \times 7 =$ _____

$5 \times 7 =$ _____

$6 \times 7 =$ _____

$7 \times 7 =$ _____

$8 \times 7 =$ _____

$9 \times 7 =$ _____

$10 \times 7 =$ _____

$1 \times 9 =$ _____

$2 \times 9 =$ _____

$3 \times 9 =$ _____

$4 \times 9 =$ _____

$5 \times 9 =$ _____

$6 \times 9 =$ _____

$7 \times 9 =$ _____

$8 \times 9 =$ _____

$9 \times 9 =$ _____

$10 \times 9 =$ _____

Week 8	Practice Page 2B

$8 \times 7 =$ _____ $3 \times 7 =$ _____ $2 \times 7 =$ _____

$7 \times 7 =$ _____ $1 \times 7 =$ _____ $4 \times 7 =$ _____

$10 \times 7 =$ _____ $9 \times 7 =$ _____ $6 \times 7 =$ _____

$5 \times 7 =$ _____ $6 \times 9 =$ _____ $9 \times 4 =$ _____

$6 \times 6 =$ _____ $9 \times 9 =$ _____ $8 \times 4 =$ _____

$5 \times 7 =$ _____ $8 \times 9 =$ _____ $5 \times 4 =$ _____

$9 \times 5 =$ _____ $10 \times 5 =$ _____ $8 \times 6 =$ _____

$3 \times 9 =$ _____ $2 \times 5 =$ _____ $6 \times 3 =$ _____

$5 \times 3 =$ _____ $8 \times 5 =$ _____ $4 \times 6 =$ _____

| Week 8 | Practice Page 3A |

1 × 7 = _____   1 × 6 = _____

2 × 7 = _____   2 × 6 = _____

3 × 7 = _____   3 × 6 = _____

4 × 7 = _____   4 × 6 = _____

5 × 7 = _____   5 × 6 = _____

6 × 7 = _____   6 × 6 = _____

7 × 7 = _____   7 × 6 = _____

8 × 7 = _____   8 × 6 = _____

9 × 7 = _____   9 × 6 = _____

10 × 7 = _____   10 × 6 = _____

Week 8	Practice Page 3B

$$
\begin{array}{ccccc}
3 & 10 & 1 & 4 & 5 \\
\times\,7 & \times\,7 & \times\,7 & \times\,7 & \times\,7 \\
\hline
\end{array}
$$

$$
\begin{array}{ccccc}
2 & 6 & 8 & 9 & 2 \\
\times\,7 & \times\,7 & \times\,7 & \times\,7 & \times\,7 \\
\hline
\end{array}
$$

$$
\begin{array}{ccccc}
4 & 8 & 3 & 6 & 2 \\
\times\,9 & \times\,4 & \times\,9 & \times\,8 & \times\,6 \\
\hline
\end{array}
$$

$$
\begin{array}{ccccc}
7 & 9 & 8 & 3 & 9 \\
\times\,10 & \times\,5 & \times\,9 & \times\,10 & \times\,9 \\
\hline
\end{array}
$$

$$
\begin{array}{ccccc}
9 & 6 & 9 & 6 & 5 \\
\times\,6 & \times\,6 & \times\,2 & \times\,10 & \times\,5 \\
\hline
\end{array}
$$

| Week 8 | Practice Page 4A |

$1 \times 7 = $ _____ $1 \times 9 = $ _____

$2 \times 7 = $ _____ $2 \times 9 = $ _____

$3 \times 7 = $ _____ $3 \times 9 = $ _____

$4 \times 7 = $ _____ $4 \times 9 = $ _____

$5 \times 7 = $ _____ $5 \times 9 = $ _____

$6 \times 7 = $ _____ $6 \times 9 = $ _____

$7 \times 7 = $ _____ $7 \times 9 = $ _____

$8 \times 7 = $ _____ $8 \times 9 = $ _____

$9 \times 7 = $ _____ $9 \times 9 = $ _____

$10 \times 7 = $ _____ $10 \times 9 = $ _____

| Week 8 | Practice Page 4B |

$1 \times 7 =$ _____ $7 \times 9 =$ _____ $6 \times 7 =$ _____

$2 \times 7 =$ _____ $10 \times 7 =$ _____ $7 \times 8 =$ _____

$7 \times 4 =$ _____ $5 \times 7 =$ _____ $7 \times 7 =$ _____

$7 \times 3 =$ _____ $9 \times 10 =$ _____ $6 \times 3 =$ _____

$4 \times 9 =$ _____ $6 \times 6 =$ _____ $5 \times 10 =$ _____

$6 \times 4 =$ _____ $7 \times 5 =$ _____ $9 \times 6 =$ _____

$8 \times 4 =$ _____ $6 \times 6 =$ _____ $9 \times 9 =$ _____

$8 \times 6 =$ _____ $8 \times 3 =$ _____ $6 \times 5 =$ _____

$7 \times 7 =$ _____ $2 \times 9 =$ _____ $6 \times 7 =$ _____

Week 8   Practice Page 5A

×	1	2	3	4	5	6	7	8	9	10
1										
2										
3										
4										
5										
6										
7										
8										
9										
10										

Week 8	Practice Page 5B

$$
\begin{array}{r} 7 \\ \times\ 7 \\ \hline \end{array}
\qquad
\begin{array}{r} 3 \\ \times\ 7 \\ \hline \end{array}
\qquad
\begin{array}{r} 5 \\ \times\ 4 \\ \hline \end{array}
\qquad
\begin{array}{r} 8 \\ \times\ 4 \\ \hline \end{array}
\qquad
\begin{array}{r} 7 \\ \times\ 2 \\ \hline \end{array}
$$

$$
\begin{array}{r} 9 \\ \times\ 6 \\ \hline \end{array}
\qquad
\begin{array}{r} 5 \\ \times\ 6 \\ \hline \end{array}
\qquad
\begin{array}{r} 1 \\ \times\ 7 \\ \hline \end{array}
\qquad
\begin{array}{r} 3 \\ \times\ 9 \\ \hline \end{array}
\qquad
\begin{array}{r} 9 \\ \times\ 9 \\ \hline \end{array}
$$

$$
\begin{array}{r} 4 \\ \times\ 3 \\ \hline \end{array}
\qquad
\begin{array}{r} 9 \\ \times\ 4 \\ \hline \end{array}
\qquad
\begin{array}{r} 6 \\ \times\ 6 \\ \hline \end{array}
\qquad
\begin{array}{r} 9 \\ \times\ 8 \\ \hline \end{array}
\qquad
\begin{array}{r} 6 \\ \times\ 7 \\ \hline \end{array}
$$

$$
\begin{array}{r} 8 \\ \times\ 6 \\ \hline \end{array}
\qquad
\begin{array}{r} 4 \\ \times\ 7 \\ \hline \end{array}
\qquad
\begin{array}{r} 5 \\ \times\ 5 \\ \hline \end{array}
\qquad
\begin{array}{r} 7 \\ \times\ 10 \\ \hline \end{array}
\qquad
\begin{array}{r} 9 \\ \times\ 4 \\ \hline \end{array}
$$

$$
\begin{array}{r} 9 \\ \times\ 7 \\ \hline \end{array}
\qquad
\begin{array}{r} 5 \\ \times\ 7 \\ \hline \end{array}
\qquad
\begin{array}{r} 4 \\ \times\ 5 \\ \hline \end{array}
\qquad
\begin{array}{r} 8 \\ \times\ 3 \\ \hline \end{array}
\qquad
\begin{array}{r} 8 \\ \times\ 7 \\ \hline \end{array}
$$

Week 9	Practice Page 1A

$1 \times 8 =$ _____ $1 \times 7 =$ _____

$2 \times 8 =$ _____ $2 \times 7 =$ _____

$3 \times 8 =$ _____ $3 \times 7 =$ _____

$4 \times 8 =$ _____ $4 \times 7 =$ _____

$5 \times 8 =$ _____ $5 \times 7 =$ _____

$6 \times 8 =$ _____ $6 \times 7 =$ _____

$7 \times 8 =$ _____ $7 \times 7 =$ _____

$8 \times 8 =$ _____ $8 \times 7 =$ _____

$9 \times 8 =$ _____ $9 \times 7 =$ _____

$10 \times 8 =$ _____ $10 \times 7 =$ _____

Week 9	Practice Page 1B

$5 \times 8 =$ _____ $8 \times 8 =$ _____ $1 \times 8 =$ _____

$10 \times 8 =$ _____ $4 \times 8 =$ _____ $9 \times 8 =$ _____

$6 \times 8 =$ _____ $3 \times 8 =$ _____ $2 \times 8 =$ _____

$7 \times 8 =$ _____ $9 \times 9 =$ _____ $7 \times 5 =$ _____

$8 \times 3 =$ _____ $3 \times 9 =$ _____ $6 \times 9 =$ _____

$6 \times 4 =$ _____ $7 \times 6 =$ _____ $9 \times 5 =$ _____

$7 \times 9 =$ _____ $4 \times 7 =$ _____ $6 \times 6 =$ _____

$4 \times 9 =$ _____ $7 \times 7 =$ _____ $4 \times 8 =$ _____

$7 \times 10 =$ _____ $5 \times 9 =$ _____ $8 \times 6 =$ _____

Week 9	Practice Page 2A

$1 \times 8 =$ _____ $1 \times 9 =$ _____

$2 \times 8 =$ _____ $2 \times 9 =$ _____

$3 \times 8 =$ _____ $3 \times 9 =$ _____

$4 \times 8 =$ _____ $4 \times 9 =$ _____

$5 \times 8 =$ _____ $5 \times 9 =$ _____

$6 \times 8 =$ _____ $6 \times 9 =$ _____

$7 \times 8 =$ _____ $7 \times 9 =$ _____

$8 \times 8 =$ _____ $8 \times 9 =$ _____

$9 \times 8 =$ _____ $9 \times 9 =$ _____

$10 \times 8 =$ _____ $10 \times 9 =$ _____

Week 9	Practice Page 2B

$8 \times 8 =$ _____ $3 \times 8 =$ _____ $2 \times 8 =$ _____

$7 \times 8 =$ _____ $1 \times 8 =$ _____ $4 \times 8 =$ _____

$10 \times 8 =$ _____ $9 \times 8 =$ _____ $6 \times 8 =$ _____

$5 \times 8 =$ _____ $5 \times 7 =$ _____ $10 \times 5 =$ _____

$7 \times 6 =$ _____ $5 \times 9 =$ _____ $8 \times 4 =$ _____

$6 \times 9 =$ _____ $3 \times 7 =$ _____ $9 \times 7 =$ _____

$7 \times 7 =$ _____ $10 \times 6 =$ _____ $7 \times 4 =$ _____

$3 \times 9 =$ _____ $9 \times 9 =$ _____ $10 \times 10 =$ _____

$6 \times 6 =$ _____ $9 \times 5 =$ _____ $6 \times 5 =$ _____

Week 9	Practice Page 3A

$1 \times 8 =$ _____ $1 \times 7 =$ _____

$2 \times 8 =$ _____ $2 \times 7 =$ _____

$3 \times 8 =$ _____ $3 \times 7 =$ _____

$4 \times 8 =$ _____ $4 \times 7 =$ _____

$5 \times 8 =$ _____ $5 \times 7 =$ _____

$6 \times 8 =$ _____ $6 \times 7 =$ _____

$7 \times 8 =$ _____ $7 \times 7 =$ _____

$8 \times 8 =$ _____ $8 \times 7 =$ _____

$9 \times 8 =$ _____ $9 \times 7 =$ _____

$10 \times 8 =$ _____ $10 \times 7 =$ _____

Week 9	Practice Page 3B

$$\begin{array}{r} 2 \\ \times\ 8 \\ \hline \end{array} \qquad \begin{array}{r} 1 \\ \times\ 8 \\ \hline \end{array} \qquad \begin{array}{r} 10 \\ \times\ 8 \\ \hline \end{array} \qquad \begin{array}{r} 5 \\ \times\ 8 \\ \hline \end{array} \qquad \begin{array}{r} 4 \\ \times\ 8 \\ \hline \end{array}$$

$$\begin{array}{r} 7 \\ \times\ 8 \\ \hline \end{array} \qquad \begin{array}{r} 6 \\ \times\ 8 \\ \hline \end{array} \qquad \begin{array}{r} 9 \\ \times\ 8 \\ \hline \end{array} \qquad \begin{array}{r} 8 \\ \times\ 8 \\ \hline \end{array} \qquad \begin{array}{r} 3 \\ \times\ 8 \\ \hline \end{array}$$

$$\begin{array}{r} 7 \\ \times\ 9 \\ \hline \end{array} \qquad \begin{array}{r} 7 \\ \times\ 4 \\ \hline \end{array} \qquad \begin{array}{r} 9 \\ \times\ 5 \\ \hline \end{array} \qquad \begin{array}{r} 7 \\ \times\ 7 \\ \hline \end{array} \qquad \begin{array}{r} 6 \\ \times\ 3 \\ \hline \end{array}$$

$$\begin{array}{r} 9 \\ \times\ 6 \\ \hline \end{array} \qquad \begin{array}{r} 5 \\ \times\ 6 \\ \hline \end{array} \qquad \begin{array}{r} 6 \\ \times\ 6 \\ \hline \end{array} \qquad \begin{array}{r} 5 \\ \times\ 4 \\ \hline \end{array} \qquad \begin{array}{r} 5 \\ \times\ 5 \\ \hline \end{array}$$

$$\begin{array}{r} 7 \\ \times\ 6 \\ \hline \end{array} \qquad \begin{array}{r} 8 \\ \times\ 4 \\ \hline \end{array} \qquad \begin{array}{r} 4 \\ \times\ 9 \\ \hline \end{array} \qquad \begin{array}{r} 10 \\ \times\ 5 \\ \hline \end{array} \qquad \begin{array}{r} 4 \\ \times\ 6 \\ \hline \end{array}$$

| Week 9 | Practice Page 4A |

$1 \times 8 =$ _____ $1 \times 6 =$ _____

$2 \times 8 =$ _____ $2 \times 6 =$ _____

$3 \times 8 =$ _____ $3 \times 6 =$ _____

$4 \times 8 =$ _____ $4 \times 6 =$ _____

$5 \times 8 =$ _____ $5 \times 6 =$ _____

$6 \times 8 =$ _____ $6 \times 6 =$ _____

$7 \times 8 =$ _____ $7 \times 6 =$ _____

$8 \times 8 =$ _____ $8 \times 6 =$ _____

$9 \times 8 =$ _____ $9 \times 6 =$ _____

$10 \times 8 =$ _____ $10 \times 6 =$ _____

Week 9	Practice Page 4B

6 × 8 = _____   8 × 9 = _____   8 × 1 = _____

8 × 8 = _____   8 × 10= _____   2 × 8 = _____

8 × 3 = _____   8 × 5 = _____   8 × 7 = _____

8 × 4 = _____   9 × 7 = _____   4 × 7 = _____

7 × 10 = _____   9 × 9 = _____   6 × 3 = _____

5 × 3 = _____   7 × 3 = _____   7 × 7 = _____

8 × 3 = _____   5 × 7 = _____   4 × 5 = _____

6 × 6 = _____   9 × 6 = _____   3 × 7 = _____

9 × 7 = _____   10 × 4 = _____   9 × 2 = _____

Week 9	Practice Page 5A

×	1	2	3	4	5	6	7	8	9	10
1										
2										
3										
4										
5										
6										
7										
8										
9										
10										

| Week 9 | Practice Page 5B |

$$
\begin{array}{r} 7 \\ \times\ 8 \\ \hline \end{array}
\qquad
\begin{array}{r} 2 \\ \times\ 7 \\ \hline \end{array}
\qquad
\begin{array}{r} 3 \\ \times\ 3 \\ \hline \end{array}
\qquad
\begin{array}{r} 3 \\ \times\ 8 \\ \hline \end{array}
\qquad
\begin{array}{r} 8 \\ \times\ 2 \\ \hline \end{array}
$$

$$
\begin{array}{r} 8 \\ \times\ 4 \\ \hline \end{array}
\qquad
\begin{array}{r} 8 \\ \times\ 6 \\ \hline \end{array}
\qquad
\begin{array}{r} 9 \\ \times\ 9 \\ \hline \end{array}
\qquad
\begin{array}{r} 7 \\ \times\ 7 \\ \hline \end{array}
\qquad
\begin{array}{r} 6 \\ \times\ 7 \\ \hline \end{array}
$$

$$
\begin{array}{r} 1 \\ \times\ 8 \\ \hline \end{array}
\qquad
\begin{array}{r} 4 \\ \times\ 4 \\ \hline \end{array}
\qquad
\begin{array}{r} 6 \\ \times\ 6 \\ \hline \end{array}
\qquad
\begin{array}{r} 9 \\ \times\ 3 \\ \hline \end{array}
\qquad
\begin{array}{r} 4 \\ \times\ 5 \\ \hline \end{array}
$$

$$
\begin{array}{r} 9 \\ \times\ 6 \\ \hline \end{array}
\qquad
\begin{array}{r} 10 \\ \times\ 3 \\ \hline \end{array}
\qquad
\begin{array}{r} 7 \\ \times\ 9 \\ \hline \end{array}
\qquad
\begin{array}{r} 5 \\ \times\ 7 \\ \hline \end{array}
\qquad
\begin{array}{r} 9 \\ \times\ 4 \\ \hline \end{array}
$$

$$
\begin{array}{r} 7 \\ \times\ 3 \\ \hline \end{array}
\qquad
\begin{array}{r} 9 \\ \times\ 8 \\ \hline \end{array}
\qquad
\begin{array}{r} 6 \\ \times\ 10 \\ \hline \end{array}
\qquad
\begin{array}{r} 8 \\ \times\ 3 \\ \hline \end{array}
\qquad
\begin{array}{r} 8 \\ \times\ 8 \\ \hline \end{array}
$$

| Week 10 | Practice Page 1A |

$1 \times 8 =$ _____ $1 \times 7 =$ _____

$2 \times 8 =$ _____ $2 \times 7 =$ _____

$3 \times 8 =$ _____ $3 \times 7 =$ _____

$4 \times 8 =$ _____ $4 \times 7 =$ _____

$5 \times 8 =$ _____ $5 \times 7 =$ _____

$6 \times 8 =$ _____ $6 \times 7 =$ _____

$7 \times 8 =$ _____ $7 \times 7 =$ _____

$8 \times 8 =$ _____ $8 \times 7 =$ _____

$9 \times 8 =$ _____ $9 \times 7 =$ _____

$10 \times 8 =$ _____ $10 \times 7 =$ _____

| Week 10 | Practice Page 1B |

$3 \times 8 =$ _____ $6 \times 6 =$ _____ $4 \times 10 =$ _____

$3 \times 2 =$ _____ $10 \times 9 =$ _____ $7 \times 8 =$ _____

$7 \times 7 =$ _____ $5 \times 9 =$ _____ $8 \times 3 =$ _____

$10 \times 8 =$ _____ $2 \times 7 =$ _____ $3 \times 6 =$ _____

$9 \times 7 =$ _____ $6 \times 8 =$ _____ $2 \times 2 =$ _____

$9 \times 2 =$ _____ $5 \times 7 =$ _____ $6 \times 9 =$ _____

$9 \times 8 =$ _____ $10 \times 6 =$ _____ $3 \times 4 =$ _____

$2 \times 6 =$ _____ $7 \times 4 =$ _____ $6 \times 7 =$ _____

$6 \times 5 =$ _____ $9 \times 9 =$ _____ $4 \times 5 =$ _____

| Week 10 | Practice Page 2A |

$1 \times 8 =$ _____ $1 \times 9 =$ _____

$2 \times 8 =$ _____ $2 \times 9 =$ _____

$3 \times 8 =$ _____ $3 \times 9 =$ _____

$4 \times 8 =$ _____ $4 \times 9 =$ _____

$5 \times 8 =$ _____ $5 \times 9 =$ _____

$6 \times 8 =$ _____ $6 \times 9 =$ _____

$7 \times 8 =$ _____ $7 \times 9 =$ _____

$8 \times 8 =$ _____ $8 \times 9 =$ _____

$9 \times 8 =$ _____ $9 \times 9 =$ _____

$10 \times 8 =$ _____ $10 \times 9 =$ _____

Week 10	Practice Page 2B

$4 \times 5 =$ _____　　　$9 \times 9 =$ _____　　　$6 \times 4 =$ _____

$6 \times 3 =$ _____　　　$6 \times 10 =$ _____　　　$8 \times 7 =$ _____

$9 \times 6 =$ _____　　　$4 \times 7 =$ _____　　　$2 \times 8 =$ _____

$1 \times 8 =$ _____　　　$5 \times 8 =$ _____　　　$2 \times 5 =$ _____

$8 \times 6 =$ _____　　　$7 \times 6 =$ _____　　　$9 \times 10 =$ _____

$10 \times 5 =$ _____　　　$5 \times 5 =$ _____　　　$6 \times 6 =$ _____

$7 \times 9 =$ _____　　　$5 \times 3 =$ _____　　　$7 \times 10 =$ _____

$2 \times 4 =$ _____　　　$10 \times 10 =$ _____　　　$8 \times 9 =$ _____

$8 \times 8 =$ _____　　　$7 \times 7 =$ _____　　　$5 \times 2 =$ _____

| Week 10 | Practice Page 3A |

$1 \times 8 =$ _____ $1 \times 7 =$ _____

$2 \times 8 =$ _____ $2 \times 7 =$ _____

$3 \times 8 =$ _____ $3 \times 7 =$ _____

$4 \times 8 =$ _____ $4 \times 7 =$ _____

$5 \times 8 =$ _____ $5 \times 7 =$ _____

$6 \times 8 =$ _____ $6 \times 7 =$ _____

$7 \times 8 =$ _____ $7 \times 7 =$ _____

$8 \times 8 =$ _____ $8 \times 7 =$ _____

$9 \times 8 =$ _____ $9 \times 7 =$ _____

$10 \times 8 =$ _____ $10 \times 7 =$ _____

Week 10	Practice Page 3B

6 × 6	5 × 6	8 × 8	9 × 5	4 × 4
3 × 3	8 × 9	7 × 3	8 × 6	1 × 7
7 × 9	8 × 4	3 × 5	2 × 3	8 × 7
7 × 2	9 × 9	8 × 2	7 × 6	4 × 2
9 × 6	2 × 9	7 × 7	5 × 4	10 × 3

Week 10	Practice Page 4A

$1 \times 8 = $ _____ $1 \times 10 = $ _____

$2 \times 8 = $ _____ $2 \times 10 = $ _____

$3 \times 8 = $ _____ $3 \times 10 = $ _____

$4 \times 8 = $ _____ $4 \times 10 = $ _____

$5 \times 8 = $ _____ $5 \times 10 = $ _____

$6 \times 8 = $ _____ $6 \times 10 = $ _____

$7 \times 8 = $ _____ $7 \times 10 = $ _____

$8 \times 8 = $ _____ $8 \times 10 = $ _____

$9 \times 8 = $ _____ $9 \times 10 = $ _____

$10 \times 8 = $ _____ $10 \times 10 = $ _____

Week 10	Practice Page 4B

$5 \times 10 =$ _____ $8 \times 8 =$ _____ $9 \times 4 =$ _____

$8 \times 5 =$ _____ $4 \times 3 =$ _____ $7 \times 7 =$ _____

$7 \times 8 =$ _____ $4 \times 6 =$ _____ $6 \times 9 =$ _____

$3 \times 10 =$ _____ $8 \times 10 =$ _____ $7 \times 5 =$ _____

$9 \times 8 =$ _____ $6 \times 6 =$ _____ $3 \times 8 =$ _____

$10 \times 2 =$ _____ $6 \times 2 =$ _____ $6 \times 8 =$ _____

$9 \times 7 =$ _____ $3 \times 9 =$ _____ $6 \times 5 =$ _____

$3 \times 7 =$ _____ $4 \times 8 =$ _____ $9 \times 9 =$ _____

$10 \times 7 =$ _____ $6 \times 7 =$ _____ $3 \times 2 =$ _____

Week 10 **Practice Page 5A**

×	1	2	3	4	5	6	7	8	9	10
1										
2										
3										
4										
5										
6										
7										
8										
9										
10										

Week 10			Practice Page 5B

$$
\begin{array}{r} 7 \\ \times\ 6 \\ \hline \end{array}
\qquad
\begin{array}{r} 10 \\ \times\ 10 \\ \hline \end{array}
\qquad
\begin{array}{r} 7 \\ \times\ 7 \\ \hline \end{array}
\qquad
\begin{array}{r} 2 \\ \times\ 7 \\ \hline \end{array}
\qquad
\begin{array}{r} 5 \\ \times\ 7 \\ \hline \end{array}
$$

$$
\begin{array}{r} 6 \\ \times\ 10 \\ \hline \end{array}
\qquad
\begin{array}{r} 8 \\ \times\ 8 \\ \hline \end{array}
\qquad
\begin{array}{r} 7 \\ \times\ 4 \\ \hline \end{array}
\qquad
\begin{array}{r} 8 \\ \times\ 9 \\ \hline \end{array}
\qquad
\begin{array}{r} 10 \\ \times\ 4 \\ \hline \end{array}
$$

$$
\begin{array}{r} 8 \\ \times\ 7 \\ \hline \end{array}
\qquad
\begin{array}{r} 9 \\ \times\ 3 \\ \hline \end{array}
\qquad
\begin{array}{r} 1 \\ \times\ 10 \\ \hline \end{array}
\qquad
\begin{array}{r} 4 \\ \times\ 9 \\ \hline \end{array}
\qquad
\begin{array}{r} 6 \\ \times\ 8 \\ \hline \end{array}
$$

$$
\begin{array}{r} 2 \\ \times\ 10 \\ \hline \end{array}
\qquad
\begin{array}{r} 6 \\ \times\ 6 \\ \hline \end{array}
\qquad
\begin{array}{r} 8 \\ \times\ 3 \\ \hline \end{array}
\qquad
\begin{array}{r} 9 \\ \times\ 9 \\ \hline \end{array}
\qquad
\begin{array}{r} 3 \\ \times\ 6 \\ \hline \end{array}
$$

$$
\begin{array}{r} 9 \\ \times\ 6 \\ \hline \end{array}
\qquad
\begin{array}{r} 4 \\ \times\ 5 \\ \hline \end{array}
\qquad
\begin{array}{r} 7 \\ \times\ 9 \\ \hline \end{array}
\qquad
\begin{array}{r} 6 \\ \times\ 4 \\ \hline \end{array}
\qquad
\begin{array}{r} 5 \\ \times\ 8 \\ \hline \end{array}
$$

ANSWER KEYS

Week 1   Practice Page 1A

$1 \times 2 =$ ___2___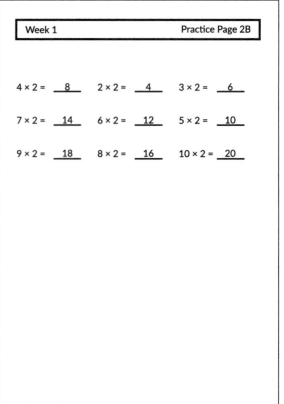

$2 \times 2 =$ ___4___

$3 \times 2 =$ ___6___

$4 \times 2 =$ ___8___

$5 \times 2 =$ ___10___

$6 \times 2 =$ ___12___

$7 \times 2 =$ ___14___

$8 \times 2 =$ ___16___

$9 \times 2 =$ ___18___

$10 \times 2 =$ ___20___

Week 1   Practice Page 1B

$3 \times 2 =$ ___6___ $2 \times 2 =$ ___4___ $4 \times 2 =$ ___8___

$5 \times 2 =$ ___10___ $6 \times 2 =$ ___12___ $8 \times 2 =$ ___16___

$10 \times 2 =$ ___20___ $7 \times 2 =$ ___14___ $9 \times 2 =$ ___18___

Week 1   Practice Page 2A

$1 \times 2 =$ ___2___

$2 \times 2 =$ ___4___

$3 \times 2 =$ ___6___

$4 \times 2 =$ ___8___

$5 \times 2 =$ ___10___

$6 \times 2 =$ ___12___

$7 \times 2 =$ ___14___

$8 \times 2 =$ ___16___

$9 \times 2 =$ ___18___

$10 \times 2 =$ ___20___

Week 1   Practice Page 2B

$4 \times 2 =$ ___8___ $2 \times 2 =$ ___4___ $3 \times 2 =$ ___6___

$7 \times 2 =$ ___14___ $6 \times 2 =$ ___12___ $5 \times 2 =$ ___10___

$9 \times 2 =$ ___18___ $8 \times 2 =$ ___16___ $10 \times 2 =$ ___20___

Week 1	Practice Page 3A

$1 \times 2 =$ __2__

$2 \times 2 =$ __4__

$3 \times 2 =$ __6__

$4 \times 2 =$ __8__

$5 \times 2 =$ __10__

$6 \times 2 =$ __12__

$7 \times 2 =$ __14__

$8 \times 2 =$ __16__

$9 \times 2 =$ __18__

$10 \times 2 =$ __20__

Week 1	Practice Page 3B

$6 \times 2 =$ __12__	$9 \times 2 =$ __18__	$8 \times 2 =$ __16__
$5 \times 2 =$ __10__	$10 \times 2 =$ __20__	$2 \times 2 =$ __4__
$4 \times 2 =$ __8__	$7 \times 2 =$ __14__	$3 \times 2 =$ __6__
$2 \times 7 =$ __14__	$2 \times 2 =$ __4__	$2 \times 8 =$ __16__
$2 \times 10 =$ __20__	$2 \times 9 =$ __18__	$2 \times 3 =$ __6__
$2 \times 6 =$ __12__	$2 \times 4 =$ __8__	$2 \times 5 =$ __10__

Week 1	Practice Page 4A

$1 \times 1 =$ __1__	$1 \times 2 =$ __2__
$2 \times 1 =$ __2__	$2 \times 2 =$ __4__
$3 \times 1 =$ __3__	$3 \times 2 =$ __6__
$4 \times 1 =$ __4__	$4 \times 2 =$ __8__
$5 \times 1 =$ __5__	$5 \times 2 =$ __10__
$6 \times 1 =$ __6__	$6 \times 2 =$ __12__
$7 \times 1 =$ __7__	$7 \times 2 =$ __14__
$8 \times 1 =$ __8__	$8 \times 2 =$ __16__
$9 \times 1 =$ __9__	$9 \times 2 =$ __18__
$10 \times 1 =$ __10__	$10 \times 2 =$ __20__

Week 1	Practice Page 4B

$8 \times 1 =$ __8__	$10 \times 1 =$ __10__	$9 \times 1 =$ __9__
$2 \times 1 =$ __2__	$6 \times 1 =$ __6__	$5 \times 1 =$ __5__
$10 \times 2 =$ __20__	$7 \times 1 =$ __7__	$4 \times 2 =$ __8__
$9 \times 2 =$ __18__	$8 \times 2 =$ __16__	$7 \times 2 =$ __14__
$3 \times 2 =$ __6__	$3 \times 1 =$ __3__	$4 \times 1 =$ __4__
$2 \times 2 =$ __4__	$1 \times 1 =$ __1__	$6 \times 2 =$ __12__

Week 1 — Practice Page 5A

×	1	2	3	4	5	6	7	8	9	10
1	1	2	3	4	5	6	7	8	9	10
2	2	4	6	8	10	12	14	16	18	20
3	3	6								
4	4	8								
5	5	10								
6	6	12								
7	7	14								
8	8	16								
9	9	18								
10	10	20								

Week 1 — Practice Page 5B

$$\begin{array}{ccccc}
1 & 6 & 9 & 2 & 10 \\
\times\,2 & \times\,2 & \times\,2 & \times\,2 & \times\,2 \\
\hline
2 & 12 & 18 & 4 & 20
\end{array}$$

$$\begin{array}{ccccc}
3 & 4 & 8 & 5 & 7 \\
\times\,2 & \times\,2 & \times\,2 & \times\,2 & \times\,2 \\
\hline
6 & 8 & 16 & 10 & 14
\end{array}$$

$$\begin{array}{ccccc}
8 & 2 & 4 & 5 & 9 \\
\times\,1 & \times\,1 & \times\,1 & \times\,1 & \times\,1 \\
\hline
8 & 2 & 4 & 5 & 9
\end{array}$$

$$\begin{array}{ccccc}
10 & 3 & 7 & 1 & 6 \\
\times\,1 & \times\,1 & \times\,1 & \times\,1 & \times\,1 \\
\hline
10 & 3 & 7 & 1 & 6
\end{array}$$

Week 2 — Practice Page 1A

$1 \times 3 = \underline{\;3\;}$	$1 \times 2 = \underline{\;2\;}$
$2 \times 3 = \underline{\;6\;}$	$2 \times 2 = \underline{\;4\;}$
$3 \times 3 = \underline{\;9\;}$	$3 \times 2 = \underline{\;6\;}$
$4 \times 3 = \underline{\;12\;}$	$4 \times 2 = \underline{\;8\;}$
$5 \times 3 = \underline{\;15\;}$	$5 \times 2 = \underline{\;10\;}$
$6 \times 3 = \underline{\;18\;}$	$6 \times 2 = \underline{\;12\;}$
$7 \times 3 = \underline{\;21\;}$	$7 \times 2 = \underline{\;14\;}$
$8 \times 3 = \underline{\;24\;}$	$8 \times 2 = \underline{\;16\;}$
$9 \times 3 = \underline{\;27\;}$	$9 \times 2 = \underline{\;18\;}$
$10 \times 3 = \underline{\;30\;}$	$10 \times 2 = \underline{\;20\;}$

Week 2 — Practice Page 1B

$2 \times 1 = \underline{\;2\;}$ $3 \times 1 = \underline{\;3\;}$	$2 \times 2 = \underline{\;4\;}$ $3 \times 2 = \underline{\;6\;}$	$2 \times 3 = \underline{\;6\;}$ $3 \times 3 = \underline{\;9\;}$
$2 \times 4 = \underline{\;8\;}$ $3 \times 4 = \underline{\;12\;}$	$2 \times 5 = \underline{\;10\;}$ $3 \times 5 = \underline{\;15\;}$	$2 \times 6 = \underline{\;12\;}$ $3 \times 6 = \underline{\;18\;}$
$2 \times 7 = \underline{\;14\;}$ $3 \times 7 = \underline{\;21\;}$	$2 \times 8 = \underline{\;16\;}$ $3 \times 8 = \underline{\;24\;}$	$2 \times 9 = \underline{\;18\;}$ $3 \times 9 = \underline{\;27\;}$
$2 \times 10 = \underline{\;20\;}$ $3 \times 10 = \underline{\;30\;}$		

Week 2	Practice Page 2A

1 × 3 = 3   1 × 1 = 1

2 × 3 = 6   2 × 1 = 2

3 × 3 = 9   3 × 1 = 3

4 × 3 = 12   4 × 1 = 4

5 × 3 = 15   5 × 1 = 5

6 × 3 = 18   6 × 1 = 6

7 × 3 = 21   7 × 1 = 7

8 × 3 = 24   8 × 1 = 8

9 × 3 = 27   9 × 1 = 9

10 × 3 = 30   10 × 1 = 10

Week 2	Practice Page 2B

2 × 3 = 6   8 × 3 = 24   3 × 3 = 9

4 × 3 = 12   5 × 3 = 15   1 × 3 = 3

9 × 3 = 27   7 × 3 = 21   10 × 3 = 30

6 × 3 = 18   1 × 7 = 7   2 × 8 = 16

1 × 9 = 9   10 × 2 = 20   4 × 1 = 4

2 × 7 = 14   2 × 1 = 2   9 × 1 = 9

5 × 1 = 5   9 × 2 = 18   3 × 2 = 6

10 × 1 = 10   6 × 1 = 6   6 × 2 = 12

2 × 5 = 10   4 × 2 = 8   2 × 10 = 20

Week 2	Practice Page 3A

1 × 3 = 3   1 × 2 = 2

2 × 3 = 6   2 × 2 = 4

3 × 3 = 9   3 × 2 = 6

4 × 3 = 12   4 × 2 = 8

5 × 3 = 15   5 × 2 = 10

6 × 3 = 18   6 × 2 = 12

7 × 3 = 21   7 × 2 = 14

8 × 3 = 24   8 × 2 = 16

9 × 3 = 27   9 × 2 = 18

10 × 3 = 30   10 × 2 = 20

Week 2	Practice Page 3B

$$\begin{array}{r} 1 \\ \times\,3 \\ \hline 3 \end{array} \quad \begin{array}{r} 6 \\ \times\,3 \\ \hline 18 \end{array} \quad \begin{array}{r} 9 \\ \times\,3 \\ \hline 27 \end{array} \quad \begin{array}{r} 2 \\ \times\,3 \\ \hline 6 \end{array} \quad \begin{array}{r} 10 \\ \times\,3 \\ \hline 30 \end{array}$$

$$\begin{array}{r} 3 \\ \times\,3 \\ \hline 9 \end{array} \quad \begin{array}{r} 4 \\ \times\,3 \\ \hline 12 \end{array} \quad \begin{array}{r} 8 \\ \times\,3 \\ \hline 24 \end{array} \quad \begin{array}{r} 5 \\ \times\,3 \\ \hline 15 \end{array} \quad \begin{array}{r} 7 \\ \times\,3 \\ \hline 21 \end{array}$$

$$\begin{array}{r} 8 \\ \times\,2 \\ \hline 16 \end{array} \quad \begin{array}{r} 2 \\ \times\,2 \\ \hline 4 \end{array} \quad \begin{array}{r} 4 \\ \times\,1 \\ \hline 4 \end{array} \quad \begin{array}{r} 4 \\ \times\,2 \\ \hline 8 \end{array} \quad \begin{array}{r} 9 \\ \times\,2 \\ \hline 18 \end{array}$$

$$\begin{array}{r} 10 \\ \times\,1 \\ \hline 10 \end{array} \quad \begin{array}{r} 2 \\ \times\,9 \\ \hline 18 \end{array} \quad \begin{array}{r} 7 \\ \times\,2 \\ \hline 14 \end{array} \quad \begin{array}{r} 1 \\ \times\,9 \\ \hline 9 \end{array} \quad \begin{array}{r} 2 \\ \times\,6 \\ \hline 12 \end{array}$$

$$\begin{array}{r} 8 \\ \times\,1 \\ \hline 8 \end{array} \quad \begin{array}{r} 5 \\ \times\,2 \\ \hline 10 \end{array} \quad \begin{array}{r} 3 \\ \times\,2 \\ \hline 6 \end{array} \quad \begin{array}{r} 1 \\ \times\,5 \\ \hline 5 \end{array} \quad \begin{array}{r} 2 \\ \times\,10 \\ \hline 20 \end{array}$$

Week 2	Practice Page 4A

1 × 3 = __3__   1 × 1 = __1__

2 × 3 = __6__   2 × 1 = __2__

3 × 3 = __9__   3 × 1 = __3__

4 × 3 = __12__   4 × 1 = __4__

5 × 3 = __15__   5 × 1 = __5__

6 × 3 = __18__   6 × 1 = __6__

7 × 3 = __21__   7 × 1 = __7__

8 × 3 = __24__   8 × 1 = __8__

9 × 3 = __27__   9 × 1 = __9__

10 × 3 = __30__   10 × 1 = __10__

Week 2	Practice Page 4B

1 × 3 = __3__   3 × 8 = __24__   2 × 2 = __4__

4 × 2 = __8__   3 × 1 = __3__   8 × 1 = __8__

5 × 1 = __5__   6 × 2 = __12__   3 × 3 = __9__

3 × 7 = __21__   1 × 7 = __7__   2 × 8 = __16__

1 × 9 = __9__   10 × 3 = __30__   4 × 1 = __4__

2 × 7 = __14__   2 × 3 = __6__   9 × 3 = __27__

5 × 3 = __15__   9 × 2 = __18__   3 × 2 = __6__

10 × 1 = __10__   6 × 1 = __6__   6 × 3 = __18__

2 × 5 = __10__   4 × 3 = __12__   2 × 10 = __20__

Week 2	Practice Page 5A

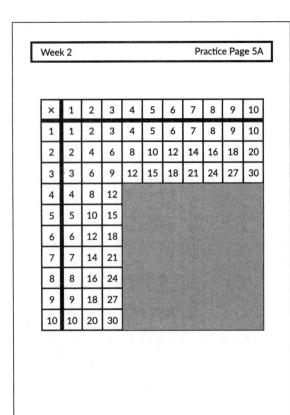

×	1	2	3	4	5	6	7	8	9	10
1	1	2	3	4	5	6	7	8	9	10
2	2	4	6	8	10	12	14	16	18	20
3	3	6	9	12	15	18	21	24	27	30
4	4	8	12							
5	5	10	15							
6	6	12	18							
7	7	14	21							
8	8	16	24							
9	9	18	27							
10	10	20	30							

Week 2	Practice Page 5B

1 × 9 = __9__   4 × 1 = __4__   10 × 3 = __30__

2 × 7 = __14__   9 × 3 = __27__   2 × 3 = __6__

5 × 3 = __15__   3 × 2 = __6__   9 × 2 = __18__

10 × 1 = __10__   6 × 3 = __18__   6 × 1 = __6__

2 × 5 = __10__   2 × 10 = __20__   4 × 3 = __12__

1 × 3 = __3__   2 × 2 = __4__   3 × 8 = __24__

4 × 2 = __8__   8 × 1 = __8__   3 × 1 = __3__

5 × 1 = __5__   3 × 3 = __9__   6 × 2 = __12__

3 × 7 = __21__   2 × 8 = __16__   1 × 7 = __7__

Week 3 Practice Page 1A

$1 \times 2 = \underline{2}$ $\quad$ $1 \times 4 = \underline{4}$

$2 \times 2 = \underline{4}$ $\quad$ $2 \times 4 = \underline{8}$

$3 \times 2 = \underline{6}$ $\quad$ $3 \times 4 = \underline{12}$

$4 \times 2 = \underline{8}$ $\quad$ $4 \times 4 = \underline{16}$

$5 \times 2 = \underline{10}$ $\quad$ $5 \times 4 = \underline{20}$

$6 \times 2 = \underline{12}$ $\quad$ $6 \times 4 = \underline{24}$

$7 \times 2 = \underline{14}$ $\quad$ $7 \times 4 = \underline{28}$

$8 \times 2 = \underline{16}$ $\quad$ $8 \times 4 = \underline{32}$

$9 \times 2 = \underline{18}$ $\quad$ $9 \times 4 = \underline{36}$

$10 \times 2 = \underline{20}$ $\quad$ $10 \times 4 = \underline{40}$

Week 3 Practice Page 1B

$2 \times 1 = \underline{2}$ $4 \times 1 = \underline{4}$	$2 \times 2 = \underline{4}$ $4 \times 2 = \underline{8}$	$2 \times 3 = \underline{6}$ $4 \times 3 = \underline{12}$
$2 \times 4 = \underline{8}$ $4 \times 4 = \underline{16}$	$2 \times 5 = \underline{10}$ $4 \times 5 = \underline{20}$	$2 \times 6 = \underline{12}$ $4 \times 6 = \underline{24}$
$2 \times 7 = \underline{14}$ $4 \times 7 = \underline{28}$	$2 \times 8 = \underline{16}$ $4 \times 8 = \underline{32}$	$2 \times 9 = \underline{18}$ $4 \times 9 = \underline{36}$
$2 \times 10 = \underline{20}$ $4 \times 10 = \underline{40}$		

Week 3 Practice Page 2A

$1 \times 4 = \underline{4}$ $\quad$ $1 \times 3 = \underline{3}$

$2 \times 4 = \underline{8}$ $\quad$ $2 \times 3 = \underline{6}$

$3 \times 4 = \underline{12}$ $\quad$ $3 \times 3 = \underline{9}$

$4 \times 4 = \underline{16}$ $\quad$ $4 \times 3 = \underline{12}$

$5 \times 4 = \underline{20}$ $\quad$ $5 \times 3 = \underline{15}$

$6 \times 4 = \underline{24}$ $\quad$ $6 \times 3 = \underline{18}$

$7 \times 4 = \underline{28}$ $\quad$ $7 \times 3 = \underline{21}$

$8 \times 4 = \underline{32}$ $\quad$ $8 \times 3 = \underline{24}$

$9 \times 4 = \underline{36}$ $\quad$ $9 \times 3 = \underline{27}$

$10 \times 4 = \underline{40}$ $\quad$ $10 \times 3 = \underline{30}$

Week 3 Practice Page 2B

$3 \times 4 = \underline{12}$ $\quad$ $9 \times 4 = \underline{36}$ $\quad$ $1 \times 4 = \underline{4}$

$6 \times 4 = \underline{24}$ $\quad$ $10 \times 4 = \underline{40}$ $\quad$ $7 \times 4 = \underline{28}$

$4 \times 4 = \underline{16}$ $\quad$ $2 \times 4 = \underline{8}$ $\quad$ $8 \times 4 = \underline{32}$

$5 \times 4 = \underline{20}$ $\quad$ $6 \times 3 = \underline{18}$ $\quad$ $3 \times 9 = \underline{27}$

$3 \times 3 = \underline{9}$ $\quad$ $2 \times 3 = \underline{6}$ $\quad$ $10 \times 3 = \underline{30}$

$8 \times 4 = \underline{32}$ $\quad$ $1 \times 4 = \underline{4}$ $\quad$ $9 \times 4 = \underline{36}$

$5 \times 2 = \underline{10}$ $\quad$ $8 \times 1 = \underline{8}$ $\quad$ $4 \times 4 = \underline{16}$

$2 \times 4 = \underline{8}$ $\quad$ $10 \times 4 = \underline{40}$ $\quad$ $6 \times 4 = \underline{24}$

$4 \times 3 = \underline{12}$ $\quad$ $6 \times 1 = \underline{6}$ $\quad$ $8 \times 3 = \underline{24}$

Week 3 — Practice Page 3A

$1 \times 4 = \underline{4}$	$1 \times 2 = \underline{2}$
$2 \times 4 = \underline{8}$	$2 \times 2 = \underline{4}$
$3 \times 4 = \underline{12}$	$3 \times 2 = \underline{6}$
$4 \times 4 = \underline{16}$	$4 \times 2 = \underline{8}$
$5 \times 4 = \underline{20}$	$5 \times 2 = \underline{10}$
$6 \times 4 = \underline{24}$	$6 \times 2 = \underline{12}$
$7 \times 4 = \underline{28}$	$7 \times 2 = \underline{14}$
$8 \times 4 = \underline{32}$	$8 \times 2 = \underline{16}$
$9 \times 4 = \underline{36}$	$9 \times 2 = \underline{18}$
$10 \times 4 = \underline{40}$	$10 \times 2 = \underline{20}$

Week 3 — Practice Page 3B

$\begin{array}{r}5\\ \times 4\\ \hline 20\end{array}$	$\begin{array}{r}10\\ \times 4\\ \hline 40\end{array}$	$\begin{array}{r}8\\ \times 4\\ \hline 32\end{array}$	$\begin{array}{r}7\\ \times 4\\ \hline 28\end{array}$	$\begin{array}{r}1\\ \times 4\\ \hline 4\end{array}$
$\begin{array}{r}4\\ \times 4\\ \hline 16\end{array}$	$\begin{array}{r}6\\ \times 4\\ \hline 24\end{array}$	$\begin{array}{r}3\\ \times 4\\ \hline 12\end{array}$	$\begin{array}{r}2\\ \times 4\\ \hline 8\end{array}$	$\begin{array}{r}9\\ \times 4\\ \hline 36\end{array}$
$\begin{array}{r}5\\ \times 3\\ \hline 15\end{array}$	$\begin{array}{r}7\\ \times 3\\ \hline 21\end{array}$	$\begin{array}{r}2\\ \times 2\\ \hline 4\end{array}$	$\begin{array}{r}3\\ \times 4\\ \hline 12\end{array}$	$\begin{array}{r}4\\ \times 2\\ \hline 8\end{array}$
$\begin{array}{r}1\\ \times 2\\ \hline 2\end{array}$	$\begin{array}{r}4\\ \times 7\\ \hline 28\end{array}$	$\begin{array}{r}2\\ \times 9\\ \hline 18\end{array}$	$\begin{array}{r}1\\ \times 3\\ \hline 3\end{array}$	$\begin{array}{r}2\\ \times 6\\ \hline 12\end{array}$
$\begin{array}{r}7\\ \times 1\\ \hline 7\end{array}$	$\begin{array}{r}10\\ \times 1\\ \hline 10\end{array}$	$\begin{array}{r}5\\ \times 4\\ \hline 20\end{array}$	$\begin{array}{r}7\\ \times 2\\ \hline 14\end{array}$	$\begin{array}{r}9\\ \times 1\\ \hline 9\end{array}$

Week 3 — Practice Page 4A

$1 \times 4 = \underline{4}$	$1 \times 3 = \underline{3}$
$2 \times 4 = \underline{8}$	$2 \times 3 = \underline{6}$
$3 \times 4 = \underline{12}$	$3 \times 3 = \underline{9}$
$4 \times 4 = \underline{16}$	$4 \times 3 = \underline{12}$
$5 \times 4 = \underline{20}$	$5 \times 3 = \underline{15}$
$6 \times 4 = \underline{24}$	$6 \times 3 = \underline{18}$
$7 \times 4 = \underline{28}$	$7 \times 3 = \underline{21}$
$8 \times 4 = \underline{32}$	$8 \times 3 = \underline{24}$
$9 \times 4 = \underline{36}$	$9 \times 3 = \underline{27}$
$10 \times 4 = \underline{40}$	$10 \times 3 = \underline{30}$

Week 3 — Practice Page 4B

$5 \times 4 = \underline{20}$	$4 \times 8 = \underline{32}$	$2 \times 4 = \underline{8}$
$4 \times 6 = \underline{24}$	$4 \times 4 = \underline{16}$	$3 \times 4 = \underline{12}$
$4 \times 10 = \underline{40}$	$1 \times 4 = \underline{4}$	$7 \times 4 = \underline{28}$
$9 \times 4 = \underline{36}$	$3 \times 1 = \underline{3}$	$2 \times 6 = \underline{12}$
$10 \times 2 = \underline{20}$	$8 \times 3 = \underline{24}$	$6 \times 1 = \underline{6}$
$3 \times 2 = \underline{6}$	$3 \times 5 = \underline{15}$	$1 \times 7 = \underline{7}$
$2 \times 1 = \underline{2}$	$4 \times 2 = \underline{8}$	$5 \times 4 = \underline{20}$
$8 \times 2 = \underline{16}$	$7 \times 3 = \underline{21}$	$10 \times 3 = \underline{30}$
$1 \times 5 = \underline{5}$	$4 \times 7 = \underline{28}$	$2 \times 7 = \underline{14}$

Week 3 — Practice Page 5A

×	1	2	3	4	5	6	7	8	9	10
1	1	2	3	4	5	6	7	8	9	10
2	2	4	6	8	10	12	14	16	18	20
3	3	6	9	12	15	18	21	24	27	30
4	4	8	12	16	20	24	28	32	36	40
5	5	10	15	20						
6	6	12	18	24						
7	7	14	21	28						
8	8	16	24	32						
9	9	18	27	36						
10	10	20	30	40						

Week 3 — Practice Page 5B

$$\begin{array}{ccccc}
9 & 3 & 8 & 6 & 7 \\
\times 4 & \times 9 & \times 2 & \times 4 & \times 3 \\
\hline
36 & 27 & 16 & 24 & 21
\end{array}$$

$$\begin{array}{ccccc}
4 & 3 & 3 & 4 & 7 \\
\times 4 & \times 3 & \times 4 & \times 2 & \times 4 \\
\hline
16 & 9 & 12 & 8 & 28
\end{array}$$

$$\begin{array}{ccccc}
2 & 8 & 4 & 2 & 5 \\
\times 2 & \times 4 & \times 1 & \times 3 & \times 4 \\
\hline
4 & 32 & 4 & 6 & 20
\end{array}$$

$$\begin{array}{ccccc}
2 & 10 & 10 & 8 & 2 \\
\times 9 & \times 2 & \times 4 & \times 3 & \times 6 \\
\hline
18 & 20 & 40 & 24 & 12
\end{array}$$

$$\begin{array}{ccccc}
6 & 3 & 5 & 5 & 2 \\
\times 3 & \times 2 & \times 2 & \times 3 & \times 7 \\
\hline
18 & 6 & 10 & 15 & 14
\end{array}$$

Week 4 — Practice Page 1A

1 × 10 = __10__	1 × 4 = __4__
2 × 10 = __20__	2 × 4 = __8__
3 × 10 = __30__	3 × 4 = __12__
4 × 10 = __40__	4 × 4 = __16__
5 × 10 = __50__	5 × 4 = __20__
6 × 10 = __60__	6 × 4 = __24__
7 × 10 = __70__	7 × 4 = __28__
8 × 10 = __80__	8 × 4 = __32__
9 × 10 = __90__	9 × 4 = __36__
10 × 10 = __100__	10 × 4 = __40__

Week 4 — Practice Page 1B

4 × 10 = __40__	8 × 10 = __80__	10 × 10 = __100__
1 × 10 = __10__	5 × 10 = __50__	9 × 10 = __90__
6 × 10 = __60__	3 × 10 = __30__	2 × 10 = __20__
7 × 10 = __70__	9 × 2 = __18__	2 × 5 = __10__
8 × 2 = __16__	3 × 9 = __27__	6 × 3 = __18__
3 × 5 = __15__	9 × 4 = __36__	7 × 3 = __21__
4 × 6 = __24__	2 × 6 = __12__	8 × 4 = __32__
10 × 2 = __20__	7 × 2 = __14__	4 × 5 = __20__
7 × 4 = __28__	10 × 3 = __30__	4 × 10 = __40__

Week 4		Practice Page 2A

$1 \times 10 = \underline{10}$ $1 \times 3 = \underline{3}$

$2 \times 10 = \underline{20}$ $2 \times 3 = \underline{6}$

$3 \times 10 = \underline{30}$ $3 \times 3 = \underline{9}$

$4 \times 10 = \underline{40}$ $4 \times 3 = \underline{12}$

$5 \times 10 = \underline{50}$ $5 \times 3 = \underline{15}$

$6 \times 10 = \underline{60}$ $6 \times 3 = \underline{18}$

$7 \times 10 = \underline{70}$ $7 \times 3 = \underline{21}$

$8 \times 10 = \underline{80}$ $8 \times 3 = \underline{24}$

$9 \times 10 = \underline{90}$ $9 \times 3 = \underline{27}$

$10 \times 10 = \underline{100}$ $10 \times 3 = \underline{30}$

Week 4		Practice Page 2B

$8 \times 10 = \underline{80}$ $3 \times 10 = \underline{30}$ $2 \times 10 = \underline{20}$

$7 \times 10 = \underline{70}$ $1 \times 10 = \underline{10}$ $4 \times 10 = \underline{40}$

$10 \times 10 = \underline{100}$ $9 \times 10 = \underline{90}$ $6 \times 10 = \underline{60}$

$5 \times 10 = \underline{50}$ $5 \times 3 = \underline{15}$ $4 \times 3 = \underline{12}$

$9 \times 2 = \underline{18}$ $2 \times 6 = \underline{12}$ $4 \times 4 = \underline{16}$

$6 \times 4 = \underline{24}$ $8 \times 4 = \underline{32}$ $4 \times 2 = \underline{8}$

$5 \times 4 = \underline{20}$ $7 \times 3 = \underline{21}$ $9 \times 4 = \underline{36}$

$3 \times 9 = \underline{27}$ $3 \times 4 = \underline{12}$ $6 \times 3 = \underline{18}$

$5 \times 2 = \underline{10}$ $4 \times 2 = \underline{8}$ $8 \times 3 = \underline{24}$

Week 4		Practice Page 3A

$1 \times 10 = \underline{10}$ $1 \times 2 = \underline{2}$

$2 \times 10 = \underline{20}$ $2 \times 2 = \underline{4}$

$3 \times 10 = \underline{30}$ $3 \times 2 = \underline{6}$

$4 \times 10 = \underline{40}$ $4 \times 2 = \underline{8}$

$5 \times 10 = \underline{50}$ $5 \times 2 = \underline{10}$

$6 \times 10 = \underline{60}$ $6 \times 2 = \underline{12}$

$7 \times 10 = \underline{70}$ $7 \times 2 = \underline{14}$

$8 \times 10 = \underline{80}$ $8 \times 2 = \underline{16}$

$9 \times 10 = \underline{90}$ $9 \times 2 = \underline{18}$

$10 \times 10 = \underline{100}$ $10 \times 2 = \underline{20}$

Week 4		Practice Page 3B

$\begin{array}{r} 3 \\ \times\,10 \\ \hline 30 \end{array}$ $\begin{array}{r} 10 \\ \times\,10 \\ \hline 100 \end{array}$ $\begin{array}{r} 1 \\ \times\,10 \\ \hline 10 \end{array}$ $\begin{array}{r} 4 \\ \times\,10 \\ \hline 40 \end{array}$ $\begin{array}{r} 5 \\ \times\,10 \\ \hline 50 \end{array}$

$\begin{array}{r} 2 \\ \times\,10 \\ \hline 20 \end{array}$ $\begin{array}{r} 6 \\ \times\,10 \\ \hline 60 \end{array}$ $\begin{array}{r} 8 \\ \times\,10 \\ \hline 80 \end{array}$ $\begin{array}{r} 9 \\ \times\,10 \\ \hline 90 \end{array}$ $\begin{array}{r} 2 \\ \times\,10 \\ \hline 20 \end{array}$

$\begin{array}{r} 7 \\ \times\,3 \\ \hline 21 \end{array}$ $\begin{array}{r} 2 \\ \times\,4 \\ \hline 8 \end{array}$ $\begin{array}{r} 3 \\ \times\,6 \\ \hline 18 \end{array}$ $\begin{array}{r} 6 \\ \times\,4 \\ \hline 24 \end{array}$ $\begin{array}{r} 3 \\ \times\,9 \\ \hline 27 \end{array}$

$\begin{array}{r} 4 \\ \times\,5 \\ \hline 20 \end{array}$ $\begin{array}{r} 8 \\ \times\,3 \\ \hline 24 \end{array}$ $\begin{array}{r} 4 \\ \times\,4 \\ \hline 16 \end{array}$ $\begin{array}{r} 10 \\ \times\,3 \\ \hline 30 \end{array}$ $\begin{array}{r} 4 \\ \times\,3 \\ \hline 12 \end{array}$

$\begin{array}{r} 8 \\ \times\,2 \\ \hline 16 \end{array}$ $\begin{array}{r} 7 \\ \times\,4 \\ \hline 28 \end{array}$ $\begin{array}{r} 8 \\ \times\,4 \\ \hline 32 \end{array}$ $\begin{array}{r} 2 \\ \times\,7 \\ \hline 14 \end{array}$ $\begin{array}{r} 5 \\ \times\,3 \\ \hline 15 \end{array}$

Week 4   Practice Page 4A

$1 \times 10 =$ _10_ $1 \times 4 =$ _4_

$2 \times 10 =$ _20_ $2 \times 4 =$ _8_

$3 \times 10 =$ _30_ $3 \times 4 =$ _12_

$4 \times 10 =$ _40_ $4 \times 4 =$ _16_

$5 \times 10 =$ _50_ $5 \times 4 =$ _20_

$6 \times 10 =$ _60_ $6 \times 4 =$ _24_

$7 \times 10 =$ _70_ $7 \times 4 =$ _28_

$8 \times 10 =$ _80_ $8 \times 4 =$ _32_

$9 \times 10 =$ _90_ $9 \times 4 =$ _36_

$10 \times 10 =$ _100_ $10 \times 4 =$ _40_

Week 4   Practice Page 4B

$1 \times 10 =$ _10_ $10 \times 9 =$ _90_ $6 \times 10 =$ _60_

$2 \times 10 =$ _20_ $10 \times 10 =$ _100_ $10 \times 8 =$ _80_

$10 \times 4 =$ _40_ $5 \times 10 =$ _50_ $7 \times 10 =$ _70_

$10 \times 3 =$ _30_ $9 \times 4 =$ _36_ $2 \times 2 =$ _4_

$8 \times 3 =$ _24_ $3 \times 3 =$ _9_ $6 \times 3 =$ _18_

$9 \times 3 =$ _27_ $8 \times 4 =$ _32_ $6 \times 4 =$ _24_

$8 \times 4 =$ _32_ $4 \times 2 =$ _8_ $9 \times 4 =$ _36_

$7 \times 3 =$ _21_ $4 \times 3 =$ _12_ $2 \times 8 =$ _16_

$4 \times 7 =$ _28_ $7 \times 4 =$ _28_ $3 \times 2 =$ _6_

Week 4   Practice Page 5A

×	1	2	3	4	5	6	7	8	9	10
1	1	2	3	4	5	6	7	8	9	10
2	2	4	6	8	10	12	14	16	18	20
3	3	6	9	12	15	18	21	24	27	30
4	4	8	12	16	20	24	28	32	36	40
5	5	10	15	20						50
6	6	12	18	24						60
7	7	14	21	28						70
8	8	16	24	32						80
9	9	18	27	36						90
10	10	20	30	40	50	60	70	80	90	100

Week 4   Practice Page 5B

$$\begin{array}{ccccc} 7 & 3 & 5 & 3 & 10 \\ \times\,10 & \times\,7 & \times\,4 & \times\,10 & \times\,2 \\ \hline 70 & 21 & 20 & 30 & 20 \end{array}$$

$$\begin{array}{ccccc} 8 & 10 & 3 & 2 & 6 \\ \times\,4 & \times\,6 & \times\,5 & \times\,9 & \times\,3 \\ \hline 32 & 60 & 15 & 18 & 18 \end{array}$$

$$\begin{array}{ccccc} 1 & 7 & 4 & 9 & 4 \\ \times\,10 & \times\,4 & \times\,4 & \times\,3 & \times\,10 \\ \hline 10 & 28 & 16 & 27 & 40 \end{array}$$

$$\begin{array}{ccccc} 4 & 10 & 8 & 10 & 9 \\ \times\,6 & \times\,3 & \times\,2 & \times\,10 & \times\,4 \\ \hline 24 & 30 & 16 & 100 & 36 \end{array}$$

$$\begin{array}{ccccc} 9 & 5 & 4 & 8 & 8 \\ \times\,10 & \times\,10 & \times\,5 & \times\,3 & \times\,10 \\ \hline 90 & 50 & 20 & 24 & 80 \end{array}$$

Week 5	Practice Page 1A

$1 \times 5 =$ __5__ $\qquad$ $1 \times 10 =$ __10__

$2 \times 5 =$ __10__ $\qquad$ $2 \times 10 =$ __20__

$3 \times 5 =$ __15__ $\qquad$ $3 \times 10 =$ __30__

$4 \times 5 =$ __20__ $\qquad$ $4 \times 10 =$ __40__

$5 \times 5 =$ __25__ $\qquad$ $5 \times 10 =$ __50__

$6 \times 5 =$ __30__ $\qquad$ $6 \times 10 =$ __60__

$7 \times 5 =$ __35__ $\qquad$ $7 \times 10 =$ __70__

$8 \times 5 =$ __40__ $\qquad$ $8 \times 10 =$ __80__

$9 \times 5 =$ __45__ $\qquad$ $9 \times 10 =$ __90__

$10 \times 5 =$ __50__ $\qquad$ $10 \times 10 =$ __100__

Week 5	Practice Page 1B

$3 \times 5 =$ __15__ $\quad$ $9 \times 5 =$ __45__ $\quad$ $1 \times 5 =$ __5__

$6 \times 5 =$ __30__ $\quad$ $10 \times 5 =$ __50__ $\quad$ $7 \times 5 =$ __35__

$4 \times 5 =$ __20__ $\quad$ $2 \times 5 =$ __10__ $\quad$ $8 \times 5 =$ __40__

$5 \times 5 =$ __25__ $\quad$ $3 \times 8 =$ __24__ $\quad$ $7 \times 2 =$ __14__

$9 \times 3 =$ __27__ $\quad$ $2 \times 10 =$ __20__ $\quad$ $9 \times 4 =$ __36__

$7 \times 4 =$ __28__ $\quad$ $5 \times 4 =$ __20__ $\quad$ $2 \times 9 =$ __18__

$3 \times 7 =$ __21__ $\quad$ $4 \times 4 =$ __16__ $\quad$ $10 \times 10 =$ __100__

$5 \times 3 =$ __15__ $\quad$ $10 \times 3 =$ __30__ $\quad$ $8 \times 2 =$ __16__

$6 \times 10 =$ __60__ $\quad$ $6 \times 3 =$ __18__ $\quad$ $4 \times 10 =$ __40__

Week 5	Practice Page 2A

$1 \times 5 =$ __5__ $\qquad$ $1 \times 3 =$ __3__

$2 \times 5 =$ __10__ $\qquad$ $2 \times 3 =$ __6__

$3 \times 5 =$ __15__ $\qquad$ $3 \times 3 =$ __9__

$4 \times 5 =$ __20__ $\qquad$ $4 \times 3 =$ __12__

$5 \times 5 =$ __25__ $\qquad$ $5 \times 3 =$ __15__

$6 \times 5 =$ __30__ $\qquad$ $6 \times 3 =$ __18__

$7 \times 5 =$ __35__ $\qquad$ $7 \times 3 =$ __21__

$8 \times 5 =$ __40__ $\qquad$ $8 \times 3 =$ __24__

$9 \times 5 =$ __45__ $\qquad$ $9 \times 3 =$ __27__

$10 \times 5 =$ __50__ $\qquad$ $10 \times 3 =$ __30__

Week 5	Practice Page 2B

$5 \times 5 =$ __25__ $\quad$ $3 \times 5 =$ __15__ $\quad$ $2 \times 5 =$ __10__

$8 \times 5 =$ __40__ $\quad$ $1 \times 5 =$ __5__ $\quad$ $4 \times 5 =$ __20__

$10 \times 5 =$ __50__ $\quad$ $9 \times 5 =$ __45__ $\quad$ $6 \times 5 =$ __30__

$7 \times 5 =$ __35__ $\quad$ $6 \times 2 =$ __12__ $\quad$ $10 \times 2 =$ __20__

$9 \times 10 =$ __90__ $\quad$ $7 \times 3 =$ __21__ $\quad$ $8 \times 3 =$ __24__

$8 \times 4 =$ __32__ $\quad$ $2 \times 8 =$ __16__ $\quad$ $3 \times 4 =$ __12__

$3 \times 3 =$ __9__ $\quad$ $7 \times 2 =$ __14__ $\quad$ $10 \times 3 =$ __30__

$6 \times 4 =$ __24__ $\quad$ $5 \times 4 =$ __20__ $\quad$ $7 \times 10 =$ __70__

$9 \times 3 =$ __27__ $\quad$ $8 \times 10 =$ __80__ $\quad$ $2 \times 9 =$ __18__

Week 5	Practice Page 3A

$1 \times 5 =$ __5__ $1 \times 10 =$ __10__

$2 \times 5 =$ __10__ $2 \times 10 =$ __20__

$3 \times 5 =$ __15__ $3 \times 10 =$ __30__

$4 \times 5 =$ __20__ $4 \times 10 =$ __40__

$5 \times 5 =$ __25__ $5 \times 10 =$ __50__

$6 \times 5 =$ __30__ $6 \times 10 =$ __60__

$7 \times 5 =$ __35__ $7 \times 10 =$ __70__

$8 \times 5 =$ __40__ $8 \times 10 =$ __80__

$9 \times 5 =$ __45__ $9 \times 10 =$ __90__

$10 \times 5 =$ __50__ $10 \times 10 =$ __100__

Week 5	Practice Page 3B

1	10	3	5	4
× 5	× 5	× 5	× 5	× 5
5	50	15	25	20

7	6	8	9	2
× 5	× 5	× 5	× 5	× 5
35	30	40	45	10

8	10	4	3	7
× 4	× 4	× 3	× 8	× 2
32	40	12	24	14

5	4	2	10	2
× 3	× 7	× 4	× 7	× 8
15	28	8	70	16

9	10	5	2	9
× 4	× 10	× 4	× 6	× 5
36	100	20	12	45

Week 5	Practice Page 4A

$1 \times 5 =$ __5__ $1 \times 4 =$ __4__

$2 \times 5 =$ __10__ $2 \times 4 =$ __8__

$3 \times 5 =$ __15__ $3 \times 4 =$ __12__

$4 \times 5 =$ __20__ $4 \times 4 =$ __16__

$5 \times 5 =$ __25__ $5 \times 4 =$ __20__

$6 \times 5 =$ __30__ $6 \times 4 =$ __24__

$7 \times 5 =$ __35__ $7 \times 4 =$ __28__

$8 \times 5 =$ __40__ $8 \times 4 =$ __32__

$9 \times 5 =$ __45__ $9 \times 4 =$ __36__

$10 \times 5 =$ __50__ $10 \times 4 =$ __40__

Week 5	Practice Page 4B

$1 \times 5 =$ __5__ $5 \times 9 =$ __45__ $6 \times 5 =$ __30__

$2 \times 5 =$ __10__ $10 \times 5 =$ __50__ $5 \times 8 =$ __40__

$5 \times 4 =$ __20__ $5 \times 5 =$ __25__ $7 \times 5 =$ __35__

$3 \times 5 =$ __15__ $9 \times 2 =$ __18__ $3 \times 9 =$ __27__

$6 \times 4 =$ __24__ $5 \times 10 =$ __50__ $3 \times 4 =$ __12__

$5 \times 7 =$ __35__ $4 \times 5 =$ __20__ $3 \times 7 =$ __21__

$10 \times 9 =$ __90__ $5 \times 5 =$ __25__ $8 \times 10 =$ __80__

$3 \times 5 =$ __15__ $8 \times 4 =$ __32__ $3 \times 3 =$ __9__

$4 \times 10 =$ __40__ $4 \times 7 =$ __28__ $4 \times 4 =$ __16__

Multiplication Facts that Stick

Week 5   Practice Page 5A

×	1	2	3	4	5	6	7	8	9	10
1	1	2	3	4	5	6	7	8	9	10
2	2	4	6	8	10	12	14	16	18	20
3	3	6	9	12	15	18	21	24	27	30
4	4	8	12	16	20	24	28	32	36	40
5	5	10	15	20	25	30	35	40	45	50
6	6	12	18	24	30					60
7	7	14	21	28	35					70
8	8	16	24	32	40					80
9	9	18	27	36	45					90
10	10	20	30	40	50	60	70	80	90	100

Week 5   Practice Page 5B

$\begin{array}{r} 8 \\ \times\,5 \\ \hline 40 \end{array}$	$\begin{array}{r} 4 \\ \times\,5 \\ \hline 20 \end{array}$	$\begin{array}{r} 8 \\ \times\,2 \\ \hline 16 \end{array}$	$\begin{array}{r} 6 \\ \times\,4 \\ \hline 24 \end{array}$	$\begin{array}{r} 10 \\ \times\,6 \\ \hline 60 \end{array}$
$\begin{array}{r} 9 \\ \times\,4 \\ \hline 36 \end{array}$	$\begin{array}{r} 3 \\ \times\,6 \\ \hline 18 \end{array}$	$\begin{array}{r} 10 \\ \times\,4 \\ \hline 40 \end{array}$	$\begin{array}{r} 8 \\ \times\,3 \\ \hline 24 \end{array}$	$\begin{array}{r} 5 \\ \times\,1 \\ \hline 5 \end{array}$
$\begin{array}{r} 5 \\ \times\,6 \\ \hline 30 \end{array}$	$\begin{array}{r} 5 \\ \times\,5 \\ \hline 25 \end{array}$	$\begin{array}{r} 10 \\ \times\,5 \\ \hline 50 \end{array}$	$\begin{array}{r} 7 \\ \times\,4 \\ \hline 28 \end{array}$	$\begin{array}{r} 5 \\ \times\,4 \\ \hline 20 \end{array}$
$\begin{array}{r} 4 \\ \times\,4 \\ \hline 16 \end{array}$	$\begin{array}{r} 10 \\ \times\,3 \\ \hline 30 \end{array}$	$\begin{array}{r} 7 \\ \times\,5 \\ \hline 35 \end{array}$	$\begin{array}{r} 5 \\ \times\,9 \\ \hline 45 \end{array}$	$\begin{array}{r} 4 \\ \times\,3 \\ \hline 12 \end{array}$
$\begin{array}{r} 3 \\ \times\,5 \\ \hline 15 \end{array}$	$\begin{array}{r} 7 \\ \times\,3 \\ \hline 21 \end{array}$	$\begin{array}{r} 4 \\ \times\,8 \\ \hline 32 \end{array}$	$\begin{array}{r} 7 \\ \times\,2 \\ \hline 14 \end{array}$	$\begin{array}{r} 9 \\ \times\,3 \\ \hline 27 \end{array}$

Week 6   Practice Page 1A

1 × 6 = 6	1 × 5 = 5
2 × 6 = 12	2 × 5 = 10
3 × 6 = 18	3 × 5 = 15
4 × 6 = 24	4 × 5 = 20
5 × 6 = 30	5 × 5 = 25
6 × 6 = 36	6 × 5 = 30
7 × 6 = 42	7 × 5 = 35
8 × 6 = 48	8 × 5 = 40
9 × 6 = 54	9 × 5 = 45
10 × 6 = 60	10 × 5 = 50

Week 6   Practice Page 1B

5 × 1 = 5	5 × 2 = 10	5 × 3 = 15
6 × 1 = 6	6 × 2 = 12	6 × 3 = 18
5 × 4 = 20	5 × 5 = 25	5 × 6 = 30
6 × 4 = 24	6 × 5 = 30	6 × 6 = 36
5 × 7 = 35	5 × 8 = 40	5 × 9 = 45
6 × 7 = 42	6 × 8 = 48	6 × 9 = 54
5 × 10 = 50		
6 × 10 = 60		

Week 6	Practice Page 2A

1 × 6 = 6	1 × 10 = 10
2 × 6= 12	2 × 10 = 20
3 × 6 = 18	3 × 10 = 30
4 × 6 = 24	4 × 10 = 40
5 × 6 = 30	5 × 10 = 50
6 × 6 = 36	6 × 10 = 60
7 × 6 = 42	7 × 10 = 70
8 × 6 = 48	8 × 10 = 80
9 × 6 = 54	9 × 10 = 90
10 × 6 = 60	10 × 10 = 100

Week 6	Practice Page 2B

5 × 6 = 30	3 × 6 = 18	2 × 6 = 12
8 × 6 = 48	1 × 6 = 6	4 × 6 = 24
10 × 6 = 60	9 × 6 = 54	6 × 6 = 36
7 × 6 = 42	9 × 4 = 36	7 × 3 = 21
5 × 7 = 35	7 × 4 = 28	9 × 5 = 45
3 × 9 = 27	8 × 4 = 32	8 × 5 = 40
5 × 5 = 25	9 × 2 = 18	10 × 3 = 30
2 × 8 = 16	5 × 10 = 50	10 × 9 = 90
5 × 4 = 20	10 × 8 = 80	8 × 3 = 24

Week 6	Practice Page 3A

1 × 6 = 6	1 × 3 = 3
2 × 6 = 12	2 × 3 = 6
3 × 6 = 18	3 × 3 = 9
4 × 6 = 24	4 × 3 = 12
5 × 6 = 30	5 × 3 = 15
6 × 6 = 36	6 × 3 = 18
7 × 6 = 42	7 × 3 = 21
8 × 6 = 48	8 × 3 = 24
9 × 6 = 54	9 × 3 = 27
10 × 6 = 60	10 × 3 = 30

Week 6	Practice Page 3B

1 × 6 6	10 × 6 60	3 × 6 18	5 × 6 30	4 × 6 24
7 × 6 42	6 × 6 36	8 × 6 48	9 × 6 54	2 × 6 12
9 × 3 27	2 × 5 10	7 × 2 14	5 × 9 45	10 × 4 40
8 × 4 32	5 × 3 15	9 × 6 54	3 × 7 21	7 × 10 70
7 × 5 35	8 × 3 24	7 × 4 28	4 × 9 36	6 × 8 48

Week 6	Practice Page 4A

1 × 6 = __6__	1 × 5 = __5__
2 × 6 = __12__	2 × 5 = __10__
3 × 6 = __18__	3 × 5 = __15__
4 × 6 = __24__	4 × 5 = __20__
5 × 6 = __30__	5 × 5 = __25__
6 × 6 = __36__	6 × 5 = __30__
7 × 6 = __42__	7 × 5 = __35__
8 × 6 = __48__	8 × 5 = __40__
9 × 6 = __54__	9 × 5 = __45__
10 × 6 = __60__	10 × 5 = __50__

Week 6	Practice Page 4B

1 × 6 = __6__	6 × 9 = __54__	6 × 6 = __36__
2 × 6 = __12__	10 × 6 = __60__	6 × 8 = __48__
6 × 4 = __24__	5 × 6 = __30__	7 × 6 = __42__
3 × 6 = __18__	10 × 8 = __80__	2 × 2 = __4__
10 × 2 = __20__	9 × 5 = __45__	10 × 4 = __40__
5 × 4 = __20__	4 × 5 = __20__	2 × 7 = __14__
8 × 5 = __40__	10 × 10 = __100__	6 × 5 = __30__
2 × 4 = __8__	8 × 2 = __16__	3 × 3 = __9__
5 × 10 = __50__	6 × 3 = __18__	4 × 6 = __24__

Week 6	Practice Page 5A

×	1	2	3	4	5	6	7	8	9	10
1	1	2	3	4	5	6	7	8	9	10
2	2	4	6	8	10	12	14	16	18	20
3	3	6	9	12	15	18	21	24	27	30
4	4	8	12	16	20	24	28	32	36	40
5	5	10	15	20	25	30	35	40	45	50
6	6	12	18	24	30	36	42	48	54	60
7	7	14	21	28	35	42				70
8	8	16	24	32	40	48				80
9	9	18	27	36	45	54				90
10	10	20	30	40	50	60	70	80	90	100

Week 6	Practice Page 5B

2 × 6 12	3 × 5 15	8 × 2 16	5 × 6 30	10 × 9 90
8 × 4 32	3 × 6 18	10 × 6 60	8 × 3 24	6 × 1 6
8 × 3 24	8 × 6 48	4 × 7 28	9 × 4 36	4 × 6 24
7 × 5 35	10 × 3 30	7 × 6 42	5 × 3 15	9 × 6 54
9 × 3 27	5 × 5 25	4 × 8 32	4 × 4 16	10 × 10 100

| Week 7 | Practice Page 1A |

1 × 9 = __9__	1 × 10 = __10__
2 × 9 = __18__	2 × 10 = __20__
3 × 9 = __27__	3 × 10 = __30__
4 × 9 = __36__	4 × 10 = __40__
5 × 9 = __45__	5 × 10 = __50__
6 × 9 = __54__	6 × 10 = __60__
7 × 9 = __63__	7 × 10 = __70__
8 × 9 = __72__	8 × 10 = __80__
9 × 9 = __81__	9 × 10 = __90__
10 × 9 = __90__	10 × 10 = __100__

| Week 7 | Practice Page 1B |

10 × 1 = __10__ 9 × 1 = __9__	10 × 2 = __20__ 9 × 2 = __18__	10 × 3 = __30__ 9 × 3 = __27__
10 × 4 = __40__ 9 × 4 = __36__	10 × 5 = __50__ 9 × 5 = __45__	10 × 6 = __60__ 9 × 6 = __54__
10 × 7 = __70__ 9 × 7 = __63__	10 × 8 = __80__ 9 × 8 = __72__	10 × 9 = __90__ 9 × 9 = __81__
10 × 10 = __100__ 9 × 10 = __90__		

| Week 7 | Practice Page 2A |

1 × 9 = __9__	1 × 6 = __6__
2 × 9 = __18__	2 × 6 = __12__
3 × 9 = __27__	3 × 6 = __18__
4 × 9 = __36__	4 × 6 = __24__
5 × 9 = __45__	5 × 6 = __30__
6 × 9 = __54__	6 × 6 = __36__
7 × 9 = __63__	7 × 6 = __42__
8 × 9 = __72__	8 × 6 = __48__
9 × 9 = __81__	9 × 6 = __54__
10 × 9 = __90__	10 × 6 = __60__

| Week 7 | Practice Page 2B |

2 × 9 = __18__	3 × 9 = __27__	8 × 9 = __72__
7 × 9 = __63__	10 × 9 = __90__	6 × 9 = __54__
1 × 9 = __9__	8 × 6 = __48__	8 × 3 = __24__
7 × 3 = __21__	4 × 8 = __32__	7 × 6 = __42__
8 × 10 = __80__	6 × 4 = __24__	7 × 4 = __28__
6 × 3 = __18__	7 × 5 = __35__	4 × 10 = __40__
5 × 5 = __25__	10 × 5 = __50__	4 × 4 = __16__
3 × 5 = __15__	8 × 2 = __16__	2 × 10 = __20__
5 × 10 = __50__	5 × 4 = __20__	6 × 5 = __30__

Week 7   Practice Page 3A

$1 \times 9 = \underline{9}$ $1 \times 4 = \underline{4}$

$2 \times 9 = \underline{18}$ $2 \times 4 = \underline{8}$

$3 \times 9 = \underline{27}$ $3 \times 4 = \underline{12}$

$4 \times 9 = \underline{36}$ $4 \times 4 = \underline{16}$

$5 \times 9 = \underline{45}$ $5 \times 4 = \underline{20}$

$6 \times 9 = \underline{54}$ $6 \times 4 = \underline{24}$

$7 \times 9 = \underline{63}$ $7 \times 4 = \underline{28}$

$8 \times 9 = \underline{72}$ $8 \times 4 = \underline{32}$

$9 \times 9 = \underline{81}$ $9 \times 4 = \underline{36}$

$10 \times 9 = \underline{90}$ $10 \times 4 = \underline{40}$

Week 7   Practice Page 3B

$\begin{array}{r} 3 \\ \times\,9 \\ \hline 27 \end{array}$	$\begin{array}{r} 10 \\ \times\,9 \\ \hline 90 \end{array}$	$\begin{array}{r} 1 \\ \times\,9 \\ \hline 9 \end{array}$	$\begin{array}{r} 4 \\ \times\,9 \\ \hline 36 \end{array}$	$\begin{array}{r} 5 \\ \times\,9 \\ \hline 45 \end{array}$
$\begin{array}{r} 2 \\ \times\,9 \\ \hline 18 \end{array}$	$\begin{array}{r} 6 \\ \times\,9 \\ \hline 54 \end{array}$	$\begin{array}{r} 8 \\ \times\,9 \\ \hline 72 \end{array}$	$\begin{array}{r} 9 \\ \times\,9 \\ \hline 81 \end{array}$	$\begin{array}{r} 2 \\ \times\,9 \\ \hline 18 \end{array}$
$\begin{array}{r} 6 \\ \times\,5 \\ \hline 30 \end{array}$	$\begin{array}{r} 6 \\ \times\,10 \\ \hline 60 \end{array}$	$\begin{array}{r} 4 \\ \times\,3 \\ \hline 12 \end{array}$	$\begin{array}{r} 7 \\ \times\,5 \\ \hline 35 \end{array}$	$\begin{array}{r} 3 \\ \times\,9 \\ \hline 27 \end{array}$
$\begin{array}{r} 7 \\ \times\,4 \\ \hline 28 \end{array}$	$\begin{array}{r} 6 \\ \times\,6 \\ \hline 36 \end{array}$	$\begin{array}{r} 8 \\ \times\,4 \\ \hline 32 \end{array}$	$\begin{array}{r} 7 \\ \times\,6 \\ \hline 42 \end{array}$	$\begin{array}{r} 7 \\ \times\,3 \\ \hline 21 \end{array}$
$\begin{array}{r} 8 \\ \times\,6 \\ \hline 48 \end{array}$	$\begin{array}{r} 7 \\ \times\,10 \\ \hline 70 \end{array}$	$\begin{array}{r} 4 \\ \times\,6 \\ \hline 24 \end{array}$	$\begin{array}{r} 5 \\ \times\,8 \\ \hline 40 \end{array}$	$\begin{array}{r} 6 \\ \times\,2 \\ \hline 12 \end{array}$

Week 7   Practice Page 4A

$1 \times 9 = \underline{9}$ $1 \times 6 = \underline{6}$

$2 \times 9 = \underline{18}$ $2 \times 6 = \underline{12}$

$3 \times 9 = \underline{27}$ $3 \times 6 = \underline{18}$

$4 \times 9 = \underline{36}$ $4 \times 6 = \underline{24}$

$5 \times 9 = \underline{45}$ $5 \times 6 = \underline{30}$

$6 \times 9 = \underline{54}$ $6 \times 6 = \underline{36}$

$7 \times 9 = \underline{63}$ $7 \times 6 = \underline{42}$

$8 \times 9 = \underline{72}$ $8 \times 6 = \underline{48}$

$9 \times 9 = \underline{81}$ $9 \times 6 = \underline{54}$

$10 \times 9 = \underline{90}$ $10 \times 6 = \underline{60}$

Week 7   Practice Page 4B

$1 \times 9 = \underline{9}$ $9 \times 9 = \underline{81}$ $6 \times 9 = \underline{54}$

$2 \times 9 = \underline{18}$ $10 \times 9 = \underline{90}$ $9 \times 8 = \underline{72}$

$9 \times 4 = \underline{36}$ $5 \times 9 = \underline{45}$ $7 \times 9 = \underline{63}$

$9 \times 3 = \underline{27}$ $3 \times 4 = \underline{12}$ $5 \times 7 = \underline{35}$

$8 \times 3 = \underline{24}$ $10 \times 4 = \underline{40}$ $4 \times 3 = \underline{12}$

$5 \times 6 = \underline{30}$ $7 \times 4 = \underline{28}$ $3 \times 3 = \underline{9}$

$10 \times 10 = \underline{100}$ $8 \times 6 = \underline{48}$ $6 \times 6 = \underline{36}$

$8 \times 4 = \underline{32}$ $7 \times 5 = \underline{35}$ $2 \times 10 = \underline{20}$

$5 \times 10 = \underline{50}$ $6 \times 3 = \underline{18}$ $4 \times 6 = \underline{24}$

Week 7 — Practice Page 5A

×	1	2	3	4	5	6	7	8	9	10
1	1	2	3	4	5	6	7	8	9	10
2	2	4	6	8	10	12	14	16	18	20
3	3	6	9	12	15	18	21	24	27	30
4	4	8	12	16	20	24	28	32	36	40
5	5	10	15	20	25	30	35	40	45	50
6	6	12	18	24	30	36	42	48	54	60
7	7	14	21	28	35	42			63	70
8	8	16	24	32	40	48		72	80
9	9	18	27	36	45	54	63	72	81	90
10	10	20	30	40	50	60	70	80	90	100

Week 7 — Practice Page 5B

7	3	7	6	9
× 9	× 8	× 3	× 7	× 2
63	24	21	42	18
8	9	6	7	3
× 6	× 6	× 6	× 4	× 10
48	54	36	28	30
4	7	8	2	4
× 2	× 5	× 4	× 5	× 5
8	35	32	10	20
4	9	8	10	9
× 6	× 3	× 10	× 9	× 4
24	27	80	90	36
9	5	6	5	8
× 9	× 9	× 5	× 3	× 9
81	45	30	15	72

Week 8 — Practice Page 1A

1 × 7 = 7	1 × 5 = 5
2 × 7 = 14	2 × 5 = 10
3 × 7 = 21	3 × 5 = 15
4 × 7 = 28	4 × 5 = 20
5 × 7 = 35	5 × 5 = 25
6 × 7 = 42	6 × 5 = 30
7 × 7 = 49	7 × 5 = 35
8 × 7 = 56	8 × 5 = 40
9 × 7 = 63	9 × 5 = 45
10 × 7 = 70	10 × 5 = 50

Week 8 — Practice Page 1B

4 × 7 = 28	8 × 7 = 56	10 × 7 = 70
1 × 7 = 7	5 × 7 = 35	9 × 7 = 63
6 × 7 = 42	3 × 7 = 21	2 × 7 = 14
7 × 7 = 49	9 × 6 = 54	8 × 4 = 32
8 × 9 = 72	6 × 6 = 36	9 × 3 = 27
8 × 6 = 48	9 × 4 = 36	7 × 3 = 21
9 × 5 = 45	9 × 9 = 81	4 × 9 = 36
7 × 5 = 35	7 × 9 = 63	4 × 10 = 40
7 × 2 = 14	10 × 10 = 100	5 × 6 = 30

Week 8	Practice Page 2A

$1 \times 7 = \underline{\ 7\ }$ $1 \times 9 = \underline{\ 9\ }$

$2 \times 7 = \underline{\ 14\ }$ $2 \times 9 = \underline{\ 18\ }$

$3 \times 7 = \underline{\ 21\ }$ $3 \times 9 = \underline{\ 27\ }$

$4 \times 7 = \underline{\ 28\ }$ $4 \times 9 = \underline{\ 36\ }$

$5 \times 7 = \underline{\ 35\ }$ $5 \times 9 = \underline{\ 45\ }$

$6 \times 7 = \underline{\ 42\ }$ $6 \times 9 = \underline{\ 54\ }$

$7 \times 7 = \underline{\ 49\ }$ $7 \times 9 = \underline{\ 63\ }$

$8 \times 7 = \underline{\ 56\ }$ $8 \times 9 = \underline{\ 72\ }$

$9 \times 7 = \underline{\ 63\ }$ $9 \times 9 = \underline{\ 81\ }$

$10 \times 7 = \underline{\ 70\ }$ $10 \times 9 = \underline{\ 90\ }$

Week 8	Practice Page 2B

$8 \times 7 = \underline{\ 56\ }$ $3 \times 7 = \underline{\ 21\ }$ $2 \times 7 = \underline{\ 14\ }$

$7 \times 7 = \underline{\ 49\ }$ $1 \times 7 = \underline{\ 7\ }$ $4 \times 7 = \underline{\ 28\ }$

$10 \times 7 = \underline{\ 70\ }$ $9 \times 7 = \underline{\ 63\ }$ $6 \times 7 = \underline{\ 42\ }$

$5 \times 7 = \underline{\ 35\ }$ $6 \times 9 = \underline{\ 54\ }$ $9 \times 4 = \underline{\ 36\ }$

$6 \times 6 = \underline{\ 36\ }$ $9 \times 9 = \underline{\ 81\ }$ $8 \times 4 = \underline{\ 32\ }$

$5 \times 7 = \underline{\ 35\ }$ $8 \times 9 = \underline{\ 72\ }$ $5 \times 4 = \underline{\ 20\ }$

$9 \times 5 = \underline{\ 45\ }$ $10 \times 5 = \underline{\ 50\ }$ $8 \times 6 = \underline{\ 48\ }$

$3 \times 9 = \underline{\ 27\ }$ $2 \times 5 = \underline{\ 10\ }$ $6 \times 3 = \underline{\ 18\ }$

$5 \times 3 = \underline{\ 15\ }$ $8 \times 5 = \underline{\ 40\ }$ $4 \times 6 = \underline{\ 24\ }$

Week 8	Practice Page 3A

$1 \times 7 = \underline{\ 7\ }$ $1 \times 6 = \underline{\ 6\ }$

$2 \times 7 = \underline{\ 14\ }$ $2 \times 6 = \underline{\ 12\ }$

$3 \times 7 = \underline{\ 21\ }$ $3 \times 6 = \underline{\ 18\ }$

$4 \times 7 = \underline{\ 28\ }$ $4 \times 6 = \underline{\ 24\ }$

$5 \times 7 = \underline{\ 35\ }$ $5 \times 6 = \underline{\ 30\ }$

$6 \times 7 = \underline{\ 42\ }$ $6 \times 6 = \underline{\ 36\ }$

$7 \times 7 = \underline{\ 49\ }$ $7 \times 6 = \underline{\ 42\ }$

$8 \times 7 = \underline{\ 56\ }$ $8 \times 6 = \underline{\ 48\ }$

$9 \times 7 = \underline{\ 63\ }$ $9 \times 6 = \underline{\ 54\ }$

$10 \times 7 = \underline{\ 70\ }$ $10 \times 6 = \underline{\ 60\ }$

Week 8	Practice Page 3B

3	10	1	4	5
$\times 7$	$\times 7$	$\times 7$	$\times 7$	$\times 7$
21	70	7	28	35

2	6	8	9	2
$\times 7$	$\times 7$	$\times 7$	$\times 7$	$\times 7$
14	42	56	63	14

4	8	3	6	2
$\times 9$	$\times 4$	$\times 9$	$\times 8$	$\times 6$
36	32	27	48	12

7	9	8	3	9
$\times 10$	$\times 5$	$\times 9$	$\times 10$	$\times 9$
70	45	72	30	81

9	6	9	6	5
$\times 6$	$\times 6$	$\times 2$	$\times 10$	$\times 5$
54	36	18	60	25

Week 8   Practice Page 4A

$1 \times 7 =$ __7__ $1 \times 9 =$ __9__

$2 \times 7 =$ __14__ $2 \times 9 =$ __18__

$3 \times 7 =$ __21__ $3 \times 9 =$ __27__

$4 \times 7 =$ __28__ $4 \times 9 =$ __36__

$5 \times 7 =$ __35__ $5 \times 9 =$ __45__

$6 \times 7 =$ __42__ $6 \times 9 =$ __54__

$7 \times 7 =$ __49__ $7 \times 9 =$ __63__

$8 \times 7 =$ __56__ $8 \times 9 =$ __72__

$9 \times 7 =$ __63__ $9 \times 9 =$ __81__

$10 \times 7 =$ __70__ $10 \times 9 =$ __90__

Week 8   Practice Page 4B

$1 \times 7 =$ __7__ $7 \times 9 =$ __63__ $6 \times 7 =$ __42__

$2 \times 7 =$ __14__ $10 \times 7 =$ __70__ $7 \times 8 =$ __56__

$7 \times 4 =$ __28__ $5 \times 7 =$ __35__ $7 \times 7 =$ __49__

$7 \times 3 =$ __21__ $9 \times 10 =$ __90__ $6 \times 3 =$ __18__

$4 \times 9 =$ __36__ $6 \times 6 =$ __36__ $5 \times 10 =$ __50__

$6 \times 4 =$ __24__ $7 \times 5 =$ __35__ $9 \times 6 =$ __54__

$8 \times 4 =$ __32__ $6 \times 6 =$ __36__ $9 \times 9 =$ __81__

$8 \times 6 =$ __48__ $8 \times 3 =$ __24__ $6 \times 5 =$ __30__

$7 \times 7 =$ __49__ $2 \times 9 =$ __18__ $6 \times 7 =$ __42__

Week 8   Practice Page 5A

×	1	2	3	4	5	6	7	8	9	10
1	1	2	3	4	5	6	7	8	9	10
2	2	4	6	8	10	12	14	16	18	20
3	3	6	9	12	15	18	21	24	27	30
4	4	8	12	16	20	24	28	32	36	40
5	5	10	15	20	25	30	35	40	45	50
6	6	12	18	24	30	36	42	48	54	60
7	7	14	21	28	35	42	49	56	63	70
8	8	16	24	32	40	48	56		72	80
9	9	18	27	36	45	54	63	72	81	90
10	10	20	30	40	50	60	70	80	90	100

Week 8   Practice Page 5B

$$\begin{array}{ccccc} 7 & 3 & 5 & 8 & 7 \\ \times\,7 & \times\,7 & \times\,4 & \times\,4 & \times\,2 \\ \hline 49 & 21 & 20 & 32 & 14 \end{array}$$

$$\begin{array}{ccccc} 9 & 5 & 1 & 3 & 9 \\ \times\,6 & \times\,6 & \times\,7 & \times\,9 & \times\,9 \\ \hline 54 & 30 & 7 & 27 & 81 \end{array}$$

$$\begin{array}{ccccc} 4 & 9 & 6 & 9 & 6 \\ \times\,3 & \times\,4 & \times\,6 & \times\,8 & \times\,7 \\ \hline 12 & 36 & 36 & 72 & 42 \end{array}$$

$$\begin{array}{ccccc} 8 & 4 & 5 & 7 & 9 \\ \times\,6 & \times\,7 & \times\,5 & \times\,10 & \times\,4 \\ \hline 48 & 28 & 25 & 70 & 36 \end{array}$$

$$\begin{array}{ccccc} 9 & 5 & 4 & 8 & 8 \\ \times\,7 & \times\,7 & \times\,5 & \times\,3 & \times\,7 \\ \hline 63 & 35 & 20 & 24 & 56 \end{array}$$

Week 9   Practice Page 1A

1 × 8 = __8__	1 × 7 = __7__
2 × 8= __16__	2 × 7= __14__
3 × 8 = __24__	3 × 7 = __21__
4 × 8 = __32__	4 × 7 = __28__
5 × 8 = __40__	5 × 7 = __35__
6 × 8 = __48__	6 × 7 = __42__
7 × 8 = __56__	7 × 7 = __49__
8 × 8 = __64__	8 × 7 = __56__
9 × 8 = __72__	9 × 7 = __63__
10 × 8 = __80__	10 × 7 = __70__

Week 9   Practice Page 1B

5 × 8 = __40__	8 × 8 = __64__	1 × 8 = __8__
10 × 8 = __80__	4 × 8 = __32__	9 × 8 = __72__
6 × 8 = __48__	3 × 8 = __24__	2 × 8 = __16__
7 × 8 = __56__	9 × 9 = __81__	7 × 5 = __35__
8 × 3 = __24__	3 × 9 = __27__	6 × 9 = __54__
6 × 4 = __24__	7 × 6 = __42__	9 × 5 = __45__
7 × 9 = __63__	4 × 7 = __28__	6 × 6 = __36__
4 × 9 = __36__	7 × 7 = __49__	4 × 8 = __32__
7 × 10 = __70__	5 × 9 = __45__	8 × 6 = __48__

Week 9   Practice Page 2A

1 × 8 = __8__	1 × 9 = __9__
2 × 8= __16__	2 × 9= __18__
3 × 8 = __24__	3 × 9 = __27__
4 × 8 = __32__	4 × 9 = __36__
5 × 8 = __40__	5 × 9 = __45__
6 × 8 = __48__	6 × 9 = __54__
7 × 8 = __56__	7 × 9 = __63__
8 × 8 = __64__	8 × 9 = __72__
9 × 8 = __72__	9 × 9 = __81__
10 × 8 = __80__	10 × 9 = __90__

Week 9   Practice Page 2B

8 × 8 = __64__	3 × 8 = __24__	2 × 8 = __16__
7 × 8 = __56__	1 × 8 = __8__	4 × 8 = __32__
10 × 8 = __80__	9 × 8 = __72__	6 × 8 = __48__
5 × 8 = __40__	5 × 7 = __35__	10 × 5 = __50__
7 × 6 = __42__	5 × 9 = __45__	8 × 4 = __32__
6 × 9 = __54__	3 × 7 = __21__	9 × 7 = __63__
7 × 7 = __49__	10 × 6 = __60__	7 × 4 = __28__
3 × 9 = __27__	9 × 9 = __81__	10 × 10 = __100__
6 × 6 = __36__	9 × 5 = __45__	6 × 5 = __30__

Week 9	Practice Page 3A

1 × 8 = __8__	1 × 7 = __7__
2 × 8 = __16__	2 × 7 = __14__
3 × 8 = __24__	3 × 7 = __21__
4 × 8 = __32__	4 × 7 = __28__
5 × 8 = __40__	5 × 7 = __35__
6 × 8 = __48__	6 × 7 = __42__
7 × 8 = __56__	7 × 7 = __49__
8 × 8 = __64__	8 × 7 = __56__
9 × 8 = __72__	9 × 7 = __63__
10 × 8 = __80__	10 × 7 = __70__

Week 9	Practice Page 3B

2	1	10	5	4
× 8	× 8	× 8	× 8	× 8
16	8	80	40	32

7	6	9	8	3
× 8	× 8	× 8	× 8	× 8
56	48	72	64	24

7	7	9	7	6
× 9	× 4	× 5	× 7	× 3
63	28	45	49	18

9	5	6	5	5
× 6	× 6	× 6	× 4	× 5
54	30	36	20	25

7	8	4	10	4
× 6	× 4	× 9	× 5	× 6
42	32	36	50	24

Week 9	Practice Page 4A

1 × 8 = __8__	1 × 6 = __6__
2 × 8 = __16__	2 × 6 = __12__
3 × 8 = __24__	3 × 6 = __18__
4 × 8 = __32__	4 × 6 = __24__
5 × 8 = __40__	5 × 6 = __30__
6 × 8 = __48__	6 × 6 = __36__
7 × 8 = __56__	7 × 6 = __42__
8 × 8 = __64__	8 × 6 = __48__
9 × 8 = __72__	9 × 6 = __54__
10 × 8 = __80__	10 × 6 = __60__

Week 9	Practice Page 4B

6 × 8 = __48__	8 × 9 = __72__	8 × 1 = __8__
8 × 8 = __64__	8 × 10 = __80__	2 × 8 = __16__
8 × 3 = __24__	8 × 5 = __40__	8 × 7 = __56__
8 × 4 = __32__	9 × 7 = __63__	4 × 7 = __28__
7 × 10 = __70__	9 × 9 = __81__	6 × 3 = __18__
5 × 3 = __15__	7 × 3 = __21__	7 × 7 = __49__
8 × 3 = __24__	5 × 7 = __35__	4 × 5 = __20__
6 × 6 = __36__	9 × 6 = __54__	3 × 7 = __21__
9 × 7 = __63__	10 × 4 = __40__	9 × 2 = __18__

Week 9									Practice Page 5A

×	1	2	3	4	5	6	7	8	9	10
1	1	2	3	4	5	6	7	8	9	10
2	2	4	6	8	10	12	14	16	18	20
3	3	6	9	12	15	18	21	24	27	30
4	4	8	12	16	20	24	28	32	36	40
5	5	10	15	20	25	30	35	40	45	50
6	6	12	18	24	30	36	42	48	54	60
7	7	14	21	28	35	42	49	56	63	70
8	8	16	24	32	40	48	56	64	72	80
9	9	18	27	36	45	54	63	72	81	90
10	10	20	30	40	50	60	70	80	90	100

Week 9   Practice Page 5B

$\begin{array}{r} 7 \\ \times\,8 \\ \hline 56 \end{array}$	$\begin{array}{r} 2 \\ \times\,7 \\ \hline 14 \end{array}$	$\begin{array}{r} 3 \\ \times\,3 \\ \hline 9 \end{array}$	$\begin{array}{r} 3 \\ \times\,8 \\ \hline 24 \end{array}$	$\begin{array}{r} 8 \\ \times\,2 \\ \hline 16 \end{array}$
$\begin{array}{r} 8 \\ \times\,4 \\ \hline 32 \end{array}$	$\begin{array}{r} 8 \\ \times\,6 \\ \hline 48 \end{array}$	$\begin{array}{r} 9 \\ \times\,9 \\ \hline 81 \end{array}$	$\begin{array}{r} 7 \\ \times\,7 \\ \hline 49 \end{array}$	$\begin{array}{r} 6 \\ \times\,7 \\ \hline 42 \end{array}$
$\begin{array}{r} 1 \\ \times\,8 \\ \hline 8 \end{array}$	$\begin{array}{r} 4 \\ \times\,4 \\ \hline 16 \end{array}$	$\begin{array}{r} 6 \\ \times\,6 \\ \hline 36 \end{array}$	$\begin{array}{r} 9 \\ \times\,3 \\ \hline 27 \end{array}$	$\begin{array}{r} 4 \\ \times\,5 \\ \hline 20 \end{array}$
$\begin{array}{r} 9 \\ \times\,6 \\ \hline 54 \end{array}$	$\begin{array}{r} 10 \\ \times\,3 \\ \hline 30 \end{array}$	$\begin{array}{r} 7 \\ \times\,9 \\ \hline 63 \end{array}$	$\begin{array}{r} 5 \\ \times\,7 \\ \hline 35 \end{array}$	$\begin{array}{r} 9 \\ \times\,4 \\ \hline 36 \end{array}$
$\begin{array}{r} 7 \\ \times\,3 \\ \hline 21 \end{array}$	$\begin{array}{r} 9 \\ \times\,8 \\ \hline 72 \end{array}$	$\begin{array}{r} 6 \\ \times\,10 \\ \hline 60 \end{array}$	$\begin{array}{r} 8 \\ \times\,3 \\ \hline 24 \end{array}$	$\begin{array}{r} 8 \\ \times\,8 \\ \hline 64 \end{array}$

Week 10   Practice Page 1A

$1 \times 8 = \underline{\ 8\ }$ $1 \times 7 = \underline{\ 7\ }$

$2 \times 8 = \underline{\ 16\ }$ $2 \times 7 = \underline{\ 14\ }$

$3 \times 8 = \underline{\ 24\ }$ $3 \times 7 = \underline{\ 21\ }$

$4 \times 8 = \underline{\ 32\ }$ $4 \times 7 = \underline{\ 28\ }$

$5 \times 8 = \underline{\ 40\ }$ $5 \times 7 = \underline{\ 35\ }$

$6 \times 8 = \underline{\ 48\ }$ $6 \times 7 = \underline{\ 42\ }$

$7 \times 8 = \underline{\ 56\ }$ $7 \times 7 = \underline{\ 49\ }$

$8 \times 8 = \underline{\ 64\ }$ $8 \times 7 = \underline{\ 56\ }$

$9 \times 8 = \underline{\ 72\ }$ $9 \times 7 = \underline{\ 63\ }$

$10 \times 8 = \underline{\ 80\ }$ $10 \times 7 = \underline{\ 70\ }$

Week 10   Practice Page 1B

$3 \times 8 = \underline{\ 24\ }$ $6 \times 6 = \underline{\ 36\ }$ $4 \times 10 = \underline{\ 40\ }$

$3 \times 2 = \underline{\ 6\ }$ $10 \times 9 = \underline{\ 90\ }$ $7 \times 8 = \underline{\ 56\ }$

$7 \times 7 = \underline{\ 49\ }$ $5 \times 9 = \underline{\ 45\ }$ $8 \times 3 = \underline{\ 24\ }$

$10 \times 8 = \underline{\ 80\ }$ $2 \times 7 = \underline{\ 14\ }$ $3 \times 6 = \underline{\ 18\ }$

$9 \times 7 = \underline{\ 63\ }$ $6 \times 8 = \underline{\ 48\ }$ $2 \times 2 = \underline{\ 4\ }$

$9 \times 2 = \underline{\ 18\ }$ $5 \times 7 = \underline{\ 35\ }$ $6 \times 9 = \underline{\ 54\ }$

$9 \times 8 = \underline{\ 72\ }$ $10 \times 6 = \underline{\ 60\ }$ $3 \times 4 = \underline{\ 12\ }$

$2 \times 6 = \underline{\ 12\ }$ $7 \times 4 = \underline{\ 28\ }$ $6 \times 7 = \underline{\ 42\ }$

$6 \times 5 = \underline{\ 30\ }$ $9 \times 9 = \underline{\ 81\ }$ $4 \times 5 = \underline{\ 20\ }$

Week 10   Practice Page 2A

1 × 8 = 8	1 × 9 = 9
2 × 8= 16	2 × 9= 18
3 × 8 = 24	3 × 9 = 27
4 × 8 = 32	4 × 9 = 36
5 × 8 = 40	5 × 9 = 45
6 × 8 = 48	6 × 9 = 54
7 × 8 = 56	7 × 9 = 63
8 × 8 = 64	8 × 9 = 72
9 × 8 = 72	9 × 9 = 81
10 × 8 = 80	10 × 9 = 90

Week 10   Practice Page 2B

4 × 5 = 20	9 × 9 = 81	6 × 4 = 24
6 × 3 = 18	6 × 10 = 60	8 × 7 = 56
9 × 6 = 54	4 × 7 = 28	2 × 8 = 16
1 × 8 = 8	5 × 8 = 40	2 × 5 = 10
8 × 6 = 48	7 × 6 = 42	9 × 10 = 90
10 × 5 = 50	5 × 5 = 25	6 × 6 = 36
7 × 9 = 63	5 × 3 = 15	7 × 10 = 70
2 × 4 = 8	10 × 10 = 100	8 × 9 = 72
8 × 8 = 64	7 × 7 = 49	5 × 2 = 10

Week 10   Practice Page 3A

1 × 8 = 8	1 × 7 = 7
2 × 8= 16	2 × 7= 14
3 × 8 = 24	3 × 7 = 21
4 × 8 = 32	4 × 7 = 28
5 × 8 = 40	5 × 7 = 35
6 × 8 = 48	6 × 7 = 42
7 × 8 = 56	7 × 7 = 49
8 × 8 = 64	8 × 7 = 56
9 × 8 = 72	9 × 7 = 63
10 × 8 = 80	10 × 7 = 70

Week 10   Practice Page 3B

6 × 6 36	5 × 6 30	8 × 8 64	9 × 5 45	4 × 4 16
3 × 3 9	8 × 9 72	7 × 3 21	8 × 6 48	1 × 7 7
7 × 9 63	8 × 4 32	3 × 5 15	2 × 3 6	8 × 7 56
7 × 2 14	9 × 9 81	8 × 2 16	7 × 6 42	4 × 2 8
9 × 6 54	2 × 9 18	7 × 7 49	5 × 4 20	10 × 3 30

Week 10   Practice Page 4A

$1 \times 8 =$ _8_ $1 \times 10 =$ _10_

$2 \times 8=$ _16_ $2 \times 10=$ _20_

$3 \times 8 =$ _24_ $3 \times 10 =$ _30_

$4 \times 8 =$ _32_ $4 \times 10 =$ _40_

$5 \times 8 =$ _40_ $5 \times 10 =$ _50_

$6 \times 8 =$ _48_ $6 \times 10 =$ _60_

$7 \times 8 =$ _56_ $7 \times 10 =$ _70_

$8 \times 8 =$ _64_ $8 \times 10 =$ _80_

$9 \times 8 =$ _72_ $9 \times 10 =$ _90_

$10 \times 8 =$ _80_ $10 \times 10 =$ _100_

Week 10   Practice Page 4B

$5 \times 10 =$ _50_ $8 \times 8 =$ _64_ $9 \times 4 =$ _36_

$8 \times 5 =$ _40_ $4 \times 3=$ _12_ $7 \times 7 =$ _49_

$7 \times 8 =$ _56_ $4 \times 6 =$ _24_ $6 \times 9 =$ _54_

$3 \times 10 =$ _30_ $8 \times 10 =$ _80_ $7 \times 5 =$ _35_

$9 \times 8 =$ _72_ $6 \times 6 =$ _36_ $3 \times 8 =$ _24_

$10 \times 2 =$ _20_ $6 \times 2 =$ _12_ $6 \times 8 =$ _48_

$9 \times 7 =$ _63_ $3 \times 9 =$ _27_ $6 \times 5 =$ _30_

$3 \times 7 =$ _21_ $4 \times 8 =$ _32_ $9 \times 9 =$ _81_

$10 \times 7 =$ _70_ $6 \times 7 =$ _42_ $3 \times 2 =$ _6_

Week 10   Practice Page 5A

×	1	2	3	4	5	6	7	8	9	10
1	1	2	3	4	5	6	7	8	9	10
2	2	4	6	8	10	12	14	16	18	20
3	3	6	9	12	15	18	21	24	27	30
4	4	8	12	16	20	24	28	32	36	40
5	5	10	15	20	25	30	35	40	45	50
6	6	12	18	24	30	36	42	48	54	60
7	7	14	21	28	35	42	49	56	63	70
8	8	16	24	32	40	48	56	64	72	80
9	9	18	27	36	45	54	63	72	81	90
10	10	20	30	40	50	60	70	80	90	100

Week 10   Practice Page 5B

7	10	7	2	5
× 6	× 10	× 7	× 7	× 7
42	100	49	14	35

6	8	7	8	10
× 10	× 8	× 4	× 9	× 4
60	64	28	72	40

8	9	1	4	6
× 7	× 3	× 10	× 9	× 8
56	27	10	36	48

2	6	8	9	3
× 10	× 6	× 3	× 9	× 6
20	36	24	81	18

9	4	7	6	5
× 6	× 5	× 9	× 4	× 8
54	20	63	24	40